D1187754

THE HISTORY OF
SQUASH RACKETS

JOHN HORRY, M.B.E.

A.C.M. WEBB (Publishing) CO. LTD.,
ENGLAND

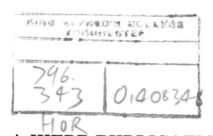
A WEBB PUBLICATION

First published in Great Britain 1979
by

A.C.M. WEBB (Publishing) CO. LTD.

33 West Street, Brighton, Sussex BN1 2 RE
England

Filmset by Jetset Limited of Brighton

Printed and bound by Planet Press Ltd, Brighton

ISBN 0 86189 007 8

THE HISTORY OF SQUASH

FOREWORD

*T*O BE a legend in your lifetime is a signal honour bestowed on only a few. In the sporting world it is normally the player who attains this distinction, but not in squash. John Horry — the administrator — the historian — the gentleman and friend of all squash players is without doubt a legend in his lifetime. Synonymous with the name of Horry is undoubtedly 4M Artillery Mansions, Victoria, London. Those of us who have been fortunate enough to imbibe in a gin and tonic at 4M, know the home of the legend.

Reclining in one of his two most comfortable armchairs, which were presented to him in recognition of his contribution to British Squash, one sees, breathes and absorbs Squash Rackets.

It is not true that John keeps the entire history of British and more recently world squash in that head of his but one only has to step inside the door of 4M to feel the nostalgia of squash history. I am positive that he has never thrown out or destroyed even one solitary envelope that contained squash information.

John Horry is encyclopaedic in his knowledge of squash and I am delighted that the world is to benefit from his knowledge in that this book will be a living memory to the father of modern squash.

Like the Squash Rackets Association of which he was Secretary for 17 years, John has been associated with squash rackets for over 50 years. His initiation to the sport had a link with the British Empire in that he had the honour of seeing HRH the Prince of Wales (later to become King Edward VIII) playing the sport in Nairobi in 1928.

John was a familiar figure at squash tournaments around London during the thirties and forties but extended his prowess to the shores of Bombay when serving in the Royal Navy. It was whilst in India that he met the legendary Hashim Khan and his cousin Abdul Bari. This chance meeting resulted in a lifetime friendship culminating in Abdul Bari becoming the first overseas player to settle in London and it was not by coincidence that he became the professional at the Junior Carlton Club.

Ten years after John's introduction to the sport he became founder and first chairman of the Middlesex SRA. During his term of office he was very much involved in the re-forming of the SRA immediately after the War. How, one is not quite sure, but during all this time he found the time and energy to serve as the Chairman of the Escorts Squash Rackets Club for some 38 years.

Although his involvement in SRA affairs began immediately after the War it was not until 1955 that he was appointed Secretary, a position he held until 1972. Upon his retirement he received the rare honour of being awarded the MBE "for services to Squash Rackets".

During the last five years of his term as Secretary of the SRA he served in the dual role of Secretary of the International Squash Rackets Federation. He continued in this capacity until 1975 when the headquarters moved to New Zealand.

His involvement in sport has not been restricted to squash as he was a regular competitor in tennis tournaments throughout England for over 25 years until his retirement from the game in 1955.

John comments that historians would have us believe that squash is merely a participant sport for the few but with its growing popularity as a spectator sport, the game is now accepted as a flourishing major sport.

With the help of sponsorship — increased press coverage — television and glass walls — the sport has become accepted as more than a recreation for the middle and upper class within exclusive clubs. It has now become one of the fastest growing sports in the western world available to all. The professional scene is growing from strength to strength and with more and more sponsors realising the potential for new markets for their products, this expansion will accelerate. This entry of commercialism will spell the doom of the distinction between professionals and amateurs and I am sure that once the administration teething problems are over, the sport will be the winner.

The enticement of prize money, the necessity for dedication and the requirement for near perfection which involves time, has lead to the word shamateurism. It is inevitable that to reach the top, the allegiance to the ideals of amateurism pale into the background. The International Olympic Committee have not accepted the inevitable yet, but it is only a matter of time before they must accept the fact that few if any, Olympic winners are true amateurs.

Commonsense and the feeling that dialogue will benefit all those associated with the sport will ensure that the transition to Open Squash will be a smooth one. The transition may not take place immediately and it is probably wise if it does not but the foundations must be layed now to ensure that no one suffers when it happens.

John has been forthright in his writing when discussing the devision in the sport between the "hardball" and "softball". Attempts have been made to see where and if compromise could be a reality, but the conclusions arrived at show that each ball has it's court. Neither ball is a success on the other court. To those not involved in the sport it is no doubt hard to believe that 30 inches in the width of a court can make such a difference to the quality of play. Both games are entrenched in their own tradition and there appears little likelihood of compromise.

John has been the world's most sought after squash rackets editor over the last 40 years and without doubt, is unrivalled in his knowledge of principal players and administrators during this time. As the current and only editor of the ISRF Handbook, I know well of his contribution to the literature of the sport. No sporting library collection will be complete without this history of squash. The fragmented history of the sport has been painstakingly pieced together to give us a comprehensive inside knowledge of the sport from its early beginnings up to the present. The pen portraits of all the famous names in squash history have given us the opportunity of feeling that they are all personal friends.

In this book John's attention to detail will enable the historians to relax with the knowledge that their work has been done for them. We are indeed fortunate that this history of the sport has been written, for without it, it may have been lost forever. The book will obviously be a must in every squash lovers library.

On behalf of all players and administrators, I salute you John for your contribution to the sport and invite all readers to savour your every word.

MURRAY C. DAY

Chairman, The International Squash Rackets Federation

1979

PREFACE

*I*N THE first fifty years of its existence, Squash Rackets was not played competitively, and was entirely unorganised. It is therefore hardly surprising that there are few references to it in contemporary literature. The game's kinship with Rackets certainly merited, but did not always obtain mention in books and articles on the older game. All of which makes extremely difficult any research into the early beginnings of Squash Rackets, and the only pictorial references are to Rackets as it was played in the Fleet Prison long before the days of squash.

The extraordinary popularity of the game today inevitably stimulates interest in its early beginnings, and it is hoped that this account of the competitive history of the game will fill a gap in the bibliography of squash.

My grateful thanks are due to my old friend Murray Day for the very generous terms in which he wrote the Foreword to this book. My thanks are also due to Mr John Gray and Mr Roy Perkins for providing some of the early illustrations, as well as to the British Squash Rackets Association through its Hon Custodian Mr Ian Wright for permission to use photographs from the SRA Library. I am also indebted to Mr Allison Danzig for his considerable help with the North American section, and to Mr. Vic Hunt for much information on Australia.

JOHN HORRY

1979

LIST OF ILLUSTRATIONS

*Reproduction rights of original material — The Rheinnardt Galleries. Reproduction prints published courtesy Rheinnardt Galleries, c/o Mr Roy Perkins, The Northwood Squash Centre Limited, Chestnut Avenue, Northwood, Middlesex, England.

CHAPTER I

HOW IT
ALL BEGAN

*I*N THE beginning was — rackets. But was that the beginning? The purist will claim that from time immemorial it has been the hobby of man to play with a ball, and the ancient Egyptians had a game with hand and ball which approximated to fives.

From fives grew real or royal tennis (court tennis in America) which flourished in French monasteries as long ago as the twelfth century. By the fifteenth century tennis had become established in England as a game for royalty and the nobility — the court built by Henry VIII at Hampton Court is still in use. By now the racket had supplanted the hand as a means of propelling the ball across a net.

That the hand was originally used at tennis is proved by the fact that the game of tennis is still, in France, called "jeu de paume" — which literally translated means the game with the hand. The balls, probably made of hide, were heavy and lifeless and could not be hit far with the bare hand, so a glove was used and then a piece of stick was inserted into the glove. Finally a short handled bat came into being and we are now in the realm of a racket. The first balls were probably made of strips of cloth rolled together and stitched with thread. Later, to increase the bounce, a leather binding was used.

The game of fives in some form or other is the oldest ball game and courts were easier and cheaper to build than tennis courts so that fives became more popular at the end of the eighteenth century. The substitution of a racket for the hand enabled the ball to be hit harder and further and this in turn led to a game which is discernable as rackets. All these games except tennis were played in the open air and rackets was originally played with only a front wall. This was the type of game played in the Fleet Prison and was described by Charles Dickens in more than one of his books including the Pickwick Papers in the late eighteen twenties. The transition to a closed court, much opposed by conservative players of those times took place between 1820 and 1850. Harrow School played Open Court rackets as early as 1822 and it was probably in the eighteen forties that the first closed court was built there.

We have now arrived at the birth of squash. The game was originally played here at Harrow by boys waiting their turn to play in the rackets court and knocking a soft ball about to get their eye in. The "court" consisted of two walls set at right angles to each other and the soft ball was used as a hard rackets ball would have been too speedy to control in the confines of the "court". No one knows exactly what type of ball was used or how big it was. The "game" caught on and several of the boarding houses at the school built courts with wooden walls and floors.

An ancestor of Judge Verney, himself an Old Harrovian and lately Chairman of the Jesters Club, in a letter written at Harrow School and dated 1850 in the possession of the Judge wrote that he had been playing 'squash'. The rackets ball moves too quickly at rackets for the novice. At squash he can learn the use of angles and court sense before embarking on the major game, so squash was probably used as a means of teaching boys rackets.

For many years the game adopted almost all the rules of rackets and was in fact frequently referred to as "mini-rackets". It had the great advantage of being cheaper to play and a squash court was also much cheaper to build and required less space. Gradually the game spread beyond the confines of Harrow School and Old Harrovians started to build wooden courts in their country houses. Boys from other schools visiting Harrow for rackets made the game's acquaintance and soon squash courts were springing up at schools all over the country.

Unfortunately there are no records of the early growth of the game, beyond an occasional reference to squash in letters. As late as 1890, in the Badminton volume of that date in an article on rackets, a mention is made quite casually of a game played with a soft ball at Harrow, and goes on to record that "there are now in existence in England several private houses with a more elaborate 'squash' court attached, built indeed like a smaller hard-ball court". The author went on to point out the advantages of this soft ball game as training for rackets. This does not correspond with the teachings of later rackets professionals who refused to allow their most promising rackets pupils to play squash for fear of harming the purity of their rackets strokes. This attitude has continued right up to the present day.

John Armitage, writing in the Lonsdale Library, Volume 16, states: "There is literally no history of Squash Rackets before 1920. Before

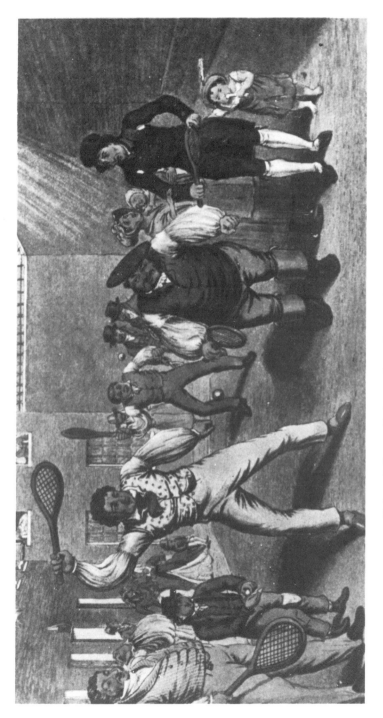

Eighteenth Century Rackets — the predecessor of Squash Rackets.

that date there was little or no play in a competitive spirit, and actually the first year of any consequence is 1922''. It was at the end of that year that the idea of an amateur championship came to be discussed. There was at this time no national body to control the sport, but the governing body of rackets, the Tennis and Rackets Association which had been formed in 1907, later appointed a sub-committee in 1922 to look after the growth of squash rackets. At this time there was a wide variety of courts in which the game was played, while the lack of governance led to an equal variety of ball and racket.

At this time a number of West End social clubs began to build courts and when the delegates from London and provincial clubs interested in squash met and decided to hold an amateur championship, one of the difficulties was what ball should be used and which court the event should be played on. A committee of six, being one from each of the six London clubs (RAC, MCC, Queens, Bath, RAF and Princes) was formed to make these decisions.

Although the sub-committee of the T and RA laid down the rules of the game, they were not prepared to undertake the administration of championships. But the delegates at the meeting which decided that an amateur championship should be held, were careful to cover themselves by adding "subject to the approval of the Tennis and Rackets Association", and from this we deduce that the T & RA through its Joint Clubs Squash Committee was regarded as the de facto governing body of the game, and this continued for another seven years until the formation of the Squash Rackets Association.

*J*UST AS the influence of the Army and the Navy had contributed to the extension of rackets to India and other parts of the world, so it was with squash. Rackets was an expensive game to play, largely because of the short life enjoyed by both rackets and balls, and the spread of squash, which was cheaper to play, contributed to the decline in the senior game especially in India where many of the rackets courts were converted into squash courts. Even at Lords, the rackets court was converted into a squash court in 1931.

The growth of squash then can be attributed to (a) The public schools; (b) The Services (and particularly the Army); (c) The West End Social Clubs.

At the time of the first amateur championship, the majority of the squash courts in England belonged to one of the above groups — the only others were the privately owned courts, mostly attached to country houses and scattered all over the country.

The growth of squash in the Nineteen Twenties was meagre and when the SRA was formed in 1929 the "Members" — there were no individual members at first — were the affiliated clubs and consisted of 14 London West End social clubs, 9 squash clubs, 5 Service Associations and establishments, 3 Sports Clubs and 5 overseas clubs. Even four years later, in 1933, the numbers had only slightly risen to

Fleet Prison, where Rackets began.

5

25 squash clubs, 18 West End social clubs, 6 Service Associations etc., 4 sports clubs, 2 schools and 16 overseas clubs. By this time individual membership of the SRA had been introduced and there were 50 members in this category. Nine county associations had also been formed.

The Thirties however saw the great pre-war squash boom and the numbers of affiliated clubs showed a dramatic increase. In the 1937-38 Handbook, the last available before the war, the number of squash clubs had leapt to 125, with 20 West End social clubs. The Services also produced 35 affiliated clubs and other organisations. The number of individual members, at 59, had shown a disappointing increase of only 9 since 1933. A large number of county organisations had been formed and at the outbreak of war in 1939 the squash outlook was distinctly promising.

*B*UT TO return to the early days. A meeting of delegates from the London and provincial clubs interested in squash rackets took place in January 1923. Dr Theodore Drysdale undertook to carry out the secretarial duties of the meetings. The relationship between this meeting, which took the title of the Squash Rackets Representative Committee, and the Tennis & Rackets Association are not at all clear, but it became evident that the T & RA while willing to let the Representative Committee undertake the details of getting an amateur championship started, and of deciding which type of ball should be used, at the same time made it perfectly clear that overall control remained with the T & RA. Moreover, although the T & RA were not represented at the first meeting Capt J. Weigall was present at a number of subsequent meetings as the representative of the T & RA. For instance, at a representatives' meeting held on 14th March it was decided that a future meeting should be held in April "with a view to sending up our final recommendations about the standardising of the court to the T & RA".

It was also the Representatives Committee who made the arrangements for the first British tour in America and subsequently initiated discussions on how to bring closer together the British and American games.

In 1926 a new body appears — the Joint Clubs Squash Racquets Committee. This appears to have been a larger body — at their meeting on 17th February in that year there were twelve members present. It is interesting to note that this committee spelt "racquets" and not "rackets" as was used by the older Representative Committee. This probably reflects the RAC influence, as the Minutes appear to have been taken by the "RAC Clerk to Committees".

It would appear that the Joint Clubs Racquets Committee superceded the Representative Committee of which no minutes are shown after those of the meeting of 18th December, 1925. The first recorded meeting of the Joint Clubs Committee seems to have been on

20th October.

The JCSRC appointed annually two representatives to sit on the committee of the T & RA, but in general the T & RA let the committee carry on unmolested with the administration of squash.

Right from the earliest days of the Representative Committee the ball problem occupied a great deal of time. Thus the minutes of the first meeting of the Committee stated that one of the objects of the meeting was ". . . to standardise balls". Col R. E. Crompton of the RAC seems to have been the ball specialist and undertook at the first meeting to provide means of weighing, measuring and comparing the bounce of the balls.

Other problems which the Committee dealt with included the standardising of the size of squash courts, and their markings, as well as the size of the rackets. Approval was given to proposals to hold new tournaments.

In March 1925 a sub-committee was appointed to report on the conditions of a Professional Championship which were to be forwarded to the T & RA. It transpired that this was to be on a challenge basis and to be played under the auspices of the T & RA.

In February 1926 a meeting was called of the "Central Squash Rackets Committee" of which the Secretary was Colonel A. Kearsey. Presumably during this meeting, but unnoticed in the Minutes, the title of the Committee was changed to the Joint Clubs Squash Racquets Committee. Nothing more was heard of the Representative Committee! Death or transfiguration must have come quickly for there is nothing in the Minutes of the last meeting of the Representative Committee on the 18th December 1925, to indicate that any change was imminent. Of the twelve members present at the last meeting of the Representative Committee, seven were at the first meeting of the JCSRC, and it seems reasonable to conclude that the latter was the same as the Representative Committee under a new name — and with possibly an enlarged membership.

$\mathcal{T}$HE COMMITTEE appeared to have power to alter the rules of the game for, at their meeting in July 1926, a proposal to alter Rule 11 was considered. This rule stated that a 'let' should be awarded if the ball having been hit by a player touched his opponent on its way to the front wall. The new proposal, which is in line with the present rule, that if the ball was travelling direct to the front wall, the striker should win the rally. It was narrowly decided that the proposed alteration should be tried out for a year. This, be it noted, without any reference to the T & RA. After a year's trial, the T & RA were asked to make permanent the proposed experimental amendment. Yet this body was asked to decide on the balls and court to be used for championships. It seems probable that the T & RA did in fact approve all the major decisions of the Committee and the absence of any recommendation to the T & RA might be attributed simply to faulty minuting by the secretary of the committee.

At this time the Committee was representative of little more than the London clubs, but efforts were made to extend the membership, first by inviting the Army and the Navy to send their representatives (but not the RAF), and later letters were sent to clubs in York, Manchester, Liverpool and Newcastle to appoint representatives.

The Bath Club Cup had been started during the 1922-23 season. At this time the Representative Committee seemed to be responsible for the conditions of the competition. Thus in September 1923 Colonel Kearsey (RAC) proposed that once a member had played for a club he should not be eligible to play for any other club as long as he remained a member of the first club. During the next three years various alterations in the conditions of the Bath Club Cup were made by the Representative Committee.

Although the administration of the Bath Club Cup occupied a not inconsiderable amount of the time of the Representative Committee it may be noted that when the Joint Clubs Committee took over the functions of the Representative Committee it had to ask the Tennis and Rackets Association to make certain changes in the Bath Club Cup Rules.

*W*HEN the SRA was formed in December 1928, its administrative problems were small. Even after five years, the number of clubs in affiliation was only just over 70 of which 16 were outside England. There were nine county associations and 50 individual members.

The Royal Automobile Club had had from the very beginning a close liaison with the SRA largely through the influence of Col W. F. Bassett, a prominent member of the RAC and Vice Chairman of the SRA. Not only were all committee meetings of the SRA held at the RAC, but the Club's Assistant Secretary, Mr Peasgood, acted as Secretary of the SRA. In four years the number of affiliated clubs had risen to 194 and 25 county associations had been formed. Moreover the SRA had become the leading national association, to which five overseas national associations and 18 overseas clubs had become affiliated. Yet the number of individual members remained disappointingly static and was only 59.

The outbreak of war in 1939 put an abrupt stop to any ideas of expansion and the SRA went into mothballs until 1946 when it was decided to reconstitute the Association. But the administrative difficulties were considerable. Mr Peasgood had unfortunately gone blind and had retired. It was decided that the duties of secretary should be undertaken by Miss Coles, Secretary to the RAC Secretary, but this lady had neither the time nor the enthusiasm necessary to give to the job and after some months it became desirable that a change should take place.

This time it was the RAC auditors who came to the rescue and Mr Duncan Fergusson, or others in his office attended meetings of committees and sub-committees and produced minutes. But these people, while anxious and willing to do their best, had not the knowledge of the game or its players to cope with the rapid expansion which was taking place in squash.

By 1948 the number of affiliated clubs had risen to 80, of which 16 were overseas, while nine overseas national associations had become affiliated. Moreover, 27 counties in England had by this time formed associations. The rapid increase in the activities of the SRA inevitably led to an increase in its expenditure and it was realised that the extra revenue needed could only be obtained by increasing the affiliation fees and the number of individual members.

This was successful to the extent that the number of individual members rose to 188 in 1948. Then it was realised that the increasing number of problems affecting all facets of the game could only be met by some form of decentralisation. This was achieved by the formation of a number of sub-committees which, while easing the work of the Executive Committee, inevitably increased the strain on Mr Fergusson and his two assistants, Mr Fry and Mr Horsefield. It was obvious that the work was becoming too much for part-timers and that even a whole time official would have his work cut out to perform successfully the many and varied duties of running the SRA.

There was also the no less formidable problem of where this official should work. Both problems were governed by the word "finance". Finally the Annual General Meeting held in June 1948 authorised the Executive Committee to find someone who would be willing to undertake this arduous task for next to nothing. To advertise such a job at the kind of salary which the SRA could afford to pay was to invite ridicule, but fortunately for the game the occasion produced the man.

Henry Hayman, a schoolmaster and Hon Secretary of the Surrey SRA, volunteered for the job. A minute room in the offices of the Federation of British Sports Goods Manufacturers just off the Haymarket was rented, and on September 1, 1948, the SRA really become independent. The RAC continued to provide accommodation for committee meetings. This was a godsend, for not more than two people could squeeze into the SRA office.

This office remained the headquarters of squash until 1961 when the landlord moved and the SRA had to find alternative accommodation. The great advantage of the Haymarket had been its central position and close proximity to the RAC where committee meetings continued to be held. It was during the SRA tenancy of this minute office that a big administrative change took place with the departure in 1955 of Henry Hayman. He had been secretary for seven years. During that time, and largely due to his untiring enthusiasm and hard work, the number of affiliated clubs had risen to 365 which included 28 overseas clubs. In addition 16 national associations had affiliated so that the SRA could rightly claim to be the world organisation of the game. In the same period the number of individual members whose subscriptions contributed the life blood of the Association had risen from 188 to 734, while there were also 123 junior members.

In spite of all the extra revenue which these affiliations and members brought in, it was barely possible for the Association to pay its way. The precarious state of the SRA finances made it impossible to employ any clerical help except at the height of the squash season when the secretary was empowered to take on a young player for two to three months. Usually young players who had represented their school or university were taken on. This had the advantage that they already knew all about squash and also knew many of the leading players. These assistants were payed the princely sum of £5 per week. They had the advantage of being able to play in the Championships and for the best clubs through which their own standard of play was enormously improved. They became a distinguished batch of players. Four (J. P. Barrington, R. M. H. Boddington, M. W. Corby and P. E. Millman) subsequently represented Great Britain, and a further four (A. P. Doggart, D. Jude, P. Richards and J. N. H. Smith) played for their country.

Very gradually, as the finances of the SRA improved and the work of the SRA expanded, their tenure of office was extended but it was not until 1969 that a whole time assistant (A. Swift) was appointed. He resigned in 1972 on his appointment as National Coach.

CHAPTER II

GROWTH AND ORGANISATION

$\mathcal{R}$ETURNING to the location of the SRA headquarters, on vacating the Haymarket a move was made to a small room kindly made available by H. J. Gray and Sons Ltd, in their showrooms in Regent Street, and this arrangement lasted until 1963 when the governing bodies of minor sports were invited by the Central Council of Physical Recreations to occupy rooms made available at their new headquarters in Park Crescent, just off Regents Park. Financial inducements by the Government by way of grants in aid of the rent etc, made it prudent to accept this offer and the SRA remained here for nine years before moving to its present HQ with the Sports Council in Knightsbridge. The progress of the SRA can be measured by the fact that this HQ consists of a large general office and four other rooms — vastly different from the ten foot square office only 12 years previously.

The clerical staff has in recent years also shown a large increase. As has already been stated, it was not until 1969 that the SRA was able to afford the luxury of a permanent assistant secretary. In addition a typist was employed for one half day a week. By 1976 the staff had risen to a secretary, an administrator, a development secretary, an affiliation secretary and five female assistants. All this in addition to the National Coach.

Who pays for all these salaries? Certainly not the SRA. This is perhaps the appropriate time to say something about its finances.

For some years after the war the two main sources of revenue were the fees paid by affiliated clubs and the individual members subscriptions. Lesser amounts were received from tournament fees, commission on sales of the architect's plans for building courts and commission and royalties on sales of publications (mainly commission on sales of "Know the Game"). In 1962 the Wolfenden Report on Sport recommended that financial aid should be given to those sports which were unable to benefit from large gates. An initial grant of £225 for the year 1962/3 was made to cover the difference between the rent already being paid for the premises in Regent Street and that in the new offices at Park Crescent, but it was in the following year that the recommendations of the Wolfenden Report began to take effect and the grant was extended to £750, of which included £500 for an assistant secretary.

In 1964 the government grant (£750) represented 31 per cent of the income of the SRA. This figure rose to 48 per cent in 1966 and thereafter fell to a minimum of 21 per cent in 1972 before rising steeply to 54 per cent in 1975.

The general rise in inflation persuaded the SRA to review the affiliation fees. Ever since the re-formaton of the SRA after the war the affiliation fee of 10s. 6d. per court had remained unaltered until 1971 when a serious deterioration in the finances of the SRA made some increase vitally necessary. The Association wanted £10 per court but this rise was considered too steep, particularly by the provincial clubs, and a compromise figure of £5 was finally, albeit reluctantly, agreed. The individual members subscription was at the same time raised from £1 1s. to £2. Many of the individual members paid by bankers orders often signed years before, and fears were expressed that the necessity of signing new bankers orders would lead to many resignations, and these were partly realised. The Association continued to receive its guinea on a bankers order form from one distinguished member for 10 years after his death!

The clubs complained that they were getting little in return for their contribution, while only the most squash-active individual members got their money's worth.

$\mathcal{T}$HE complaints regarding the rise in affiliation fees in 1971 were nothing compared to the uproar two years later when the affiliation fee per court was raised from £5 to £25. The commercial court owners, who by this time had banded themselves together to form the British Squash Rackets Proprietors Federation, were adamant that the rate was iniquitous and even unnecessary and refused to pay it. A running battle between the two bodies went on for three years before peace was restored after the SRA had made some concessions to limit the maximum amount payable by multi-court clubs.

The late CAPTAIN J. E. PALMER-TOMKINSON — First Chairman of the SRA.

13

The effect of the new rates on the finances of the SRA was certainly dramatic. The nett receipts from affiliation fees and individual members subscriptions rose from £8,000 in 1973 to £19,000 in 1975. Coupled with the large increase in Government grants one would have expected that all this would have resulted in a massive surplus, but this was not so. While a deficit of £5,042 in 1973 was transformed into a surplus of £7,509 in 1974, this gave way to a further deficit of £97 in 1975. This was largely caused by the enormous sums paid out by the SRA in salaries and expenses.

The following table is instructive:

Salaries & Expenses

1965	1973	1974	1975	1976	1977	1978
1,826	11,789	24,782	43,265	48,204	55,164	67,994

One cannot help wondering if there was not some validity in the complaints of the proprietors that there was something wrong with the administration at headquarters.

THE WAR

*T*HE WAR battered squash as it did so many other sports. It effectively stopped the construction of any new courts and the shortage of bricks in the immediate post war period resulted in a ban on court building lasting in all for nearly fifteen years. The impetus of the big boom of the early thirties was not quite maintained in the immediate pre-war years, but this is not to infer that in these years the game was stagnant. Competitively, the game in 1939 was thriving as never before. New competitions were constantly being organised. The game was gaining fresh adherants and there was no lack of entries for the Amateur Championship, although there was no qualifying competition in those days. Looking through the results of the last Amateur Championship played before the war — in December 1938 — one is struck by the very large proportion of the players who survived the war. Seventeen players who played in the 1938-9 Championship returned eight years later to play in the first Amateur Championship after the war.

War broke out just before the 1939-40 season would have started and during the next seven years there were no tournaments in England. Friendly matches — yes.

But outside England away from the theatres of war competitive squash continued to be enjoyed. I well remember being asked to organise the West of India Championship at the Cricket Club of India in Bombay in September 1944. There was a fair sprinkling of British

Service personnel playing of whom the best was Lieut-Com Alan Seymour-Haydon RN, one of the many players who were robbed of their best competitive years by the war. There was also a West of India Professional Championship and here I got my first glimpse of Hashim Khan, who, predictably, won the event beating the local pro Abdul Bari in the final.

But these tournaments were few and far between and the majority of British players had to forego serious play until after the war. Even friendly play was made difficult by the shortage of balls.

Nowhere was the ball shortage more keenly felt than in Sweden, cut off from all normal sources of supply. RAF pilots, for various reasons had to fly in on occasion, and it was standard practise that they should bring with them a box of balls — and this was the only source open to the Swedes during the whole war.

Squash was lucky in that so few courts in England were destroyed by enemy action. Among the West End social clubs, the only casualty from bombing was the Ladies Carlton Club, which possessed, apart from singles courts, one of the few precious doubles courts in London. The Bath Club, where the Amateur Championship was played prior to the war, and which in those days was in Dover Street, was burned down during the war, but not by enemy action.

Perhaps the greatest loss to the game, courtwise, was the Thames House Club. This was the largest squash club in the country at that time with 15 courts. It had an ideal situation on Millbank, only two minutes walk from the Houses of Parliament. The courts were all in the basement, and therefore rather hot, but there was a swimming pool attached to the club in which to cool off after a game. Early in the war, the courts were commandeered by the Government and used for the storage of files! After the war, strenuous efforts were made by many influential squash players to get them released but all to no avail until the Civil Service SRA who had been using the courts in Carlton House Terrace, at one time owned by the Union Club and which were scheduled for demolition, managed to get two (and later a third) of the Millbank courts released. But there are still a dozen courts languishing and waiting for the day when they will be returned to their proper use.

There were two spheres where squash flourished throughout the war — the universities and the London hospitals. Officially, there were no university matches between Oxford and Cambridge after the 1938/9 season until after the war, but unofficial matches were played and half Blues awarded. The universities resumed official matches immediately after the war and in the 1945/6 season the first post war Oxford v Cambridge match was played, for some reason, at Trenchard House on Metropolitan Police courts.

The star at the London hospitals during the war was Peter Hildick-Smith, a South African. Although at that time recognised as a good player, it did not appear as if he would develop into an Amateur Champion which he became in 1951/2, having been runner-up to

15

Norman Borrett in the previous year.

The efforts of Lieut S. G. S. Pawle RNVR to keep the competitive game alive during the war were so successful as to demand some detailed treatment. It was in September 1941 when serving at the Admiralty that Gerald Pawle conceived the idea of forming a team composed of good players from all Services who would be prepared to play matches outside as well as inside London. The RAC was one of the London Clubs which offered hospitality to Officers and this club was the base from which the team operated. During the first season, the backbone of the team consisted of the late Rex Forbes-Bassett, then a Lieutenant in the Army, Pay-Lieut-Cdr, now Captain (retired) F. V. Harrison, Lieut (A) H. J. Dagnall RNVR, Pay-Sub Lieut R. F. Whittow RNVR in addition to Gerald Pawle who captained the team.

Rapidly the team became the best side in England and in its first season won 20 out of its 21 matches. Its only defeat was at the hands of a combined Hospitals teams which won 4-1, the only winner for the losing side being Gerald Pawle, who beat Peter Hildick-Smith 9-8, 5-9, 9-7, 1-9, 9-6. Ten years later Hildick-Smith won the Amateur Championship, so it was no mean feat of Pawle's. The opposition was provided mainly by the London hospitals, but the London Fire Force and the Metropolitan Police were also played in addition to some of the London squash clubs.

In the following season, the team became more ambitious and increased their fixtures to 33, winning all but one (Guys Hospital). Whereas in the first season only 11 players had played for the team, in the 1942/3 season 21 players took part, although the original quartet of Pawle, Forbes-Bassett, Harrison and Dagnall continued to play in the team in the majority of the matches. For the first time, the Universities of Oxford and Cambridge were played — three matches against each and all were won. Even a combined Oxford and Cambridge team could not check the success of Pawle's team. Moreover the margins of victory were impressive, most of the wins being 5-0.

Suddenly in 1943 it was over, and all the regular members of the team were posted abroad. While they were together the team had done a magnificent job in keeping squash alive, and the greatest credit is due to Gerald Pawle for the initiative as well as the hard work which organising so many matches entailed.

POST WAR DEVELOPMENT

The main factor restricting the growth of post-war squash was undoubtedly the building restrictions which prevented the construction of new courts on any large scale. The partial lifting of these restrictions in 1954 gave the green light, but now the bugbear was the high cost of construction.

Another high cost which was having its effect on the game was that of travelling, but this was offset by a general raising in prosperity, and overseas tours which had been interrupted by the War began to take place again. One of the first was a first visit by New Zealand to Australia in 1953. Even in those early days of antipodean squash New Zealand were not considered strong enough to be granted Test Match status against Australia, but the visiting side gave a good account of itself when playing the state sides of Victoria, New South Wales and Queensland.

The first United States Open Championship was held at the beginning of 1954 in New York. This was the first tournament to be held in the USA which was open to amateurs and professionals of all creeds and colours. With 20 entries accepted from six overseas countries it could not be denied that representation was world wide. Although some of the 'foreigners' were by this time resident in the US others had made the journey specially to compete and had had little time to acclimatise themselves to the American game. Of such were Hashim Khan and Mahmoud Kerim, both of whom reached the semi-finals, and both beaten by Henri Salaun the US amateur champion, Kerim in the semi-final and Hashim in the final.

Although England had played international matches against Denmark in 1949 in Copenhagen and in the following year in England, these were not continued and the visit of a Netherlands side to England in December 1953 was successful when playing club sides, but the visitors were hopelessly outplayed by the full England side, and the experiment was not repeated. This does not mean that there was no competition between Dutch and English teams, but that for many years has been on a club level. The close proximity of Holland to England makes for ease in travelling and English club sides have always been made welcome in the small number of Dutch clubs operating in those far-off days.

Of the Home Counties, Wales was by far the most backward and were not given a match with England until November 1951. But the Welsh were an enterprising Association and took part in a triangular contest with Sweden and Denmark in 1954.

In the early days of the Home internationals Scotland had been the strongest team after England and international matches had started between the two countries in 1937. The England-Ireland series was commenced in February 1949 in Dublin. In the early fifties Wales had a strong team which had a run of successes against both Scotland and Ireland, while recently it has been Ireland which has had the edge over Scotland and Wales.

The big breakthrough in international competition occurred in 1955 when the first English team visited South Africa. The invitation came from South Africa in 1954 and the members of the team were assured that they would be looked after at no cost to themselves once they had landed in South Africa. This was before the days of sponsorship and

17

no Government assistance could be envisaged for a team travelling to South Africa. The SRA made an appeal for contributions to pay for part of the fares of the team of five which was originally selected. It was pointed out that to send the bare minimum of players without a reserve was to court disaster, and it is surprising that such a scheme was ever envisaged. It was done in the hope that money would thereby be saved. Fortunately wiser counsels prevailed and somehow the City provided the extra cost for a sixth player. The composition of the original team gave rise to some criticism. Norman Borrett, the Captain had played little squash during the preceding season and was over 35. Both A. Seymour-Haydon and B. C. Phillips were even older. Only Seymour-Haydon and Perkins had reached the last eight of the Amateur Championships. There were many who thought that R. B. Hawkey should have been chosen in the first place, and he was in fact chosen as the sixth member. The team was not a happy one and certain events, off as well as on court, did not improve matters. Four matches before the first Test did not give the touring team sufficient time to get accustomed to the altitude. Understandably South Africa won the first Test played at Johannesburg, but in the second Test played at sea level at Durban, the British team did much better and exactly reversed the result of the first Test.

With the third Test also being played at sea level at Cape Town, British hopes were understandably high but these were not realised, Borrett and Phillips both being extremely disappointing, and the South Africans won 3-2. To complete British humiliation, the fourth Test played back at Johannesburg was also lost by the same margin. The result of the Test series was a great shock to British squash. There is no doubt that the standard of the game in South Africa was badly underestimated, and the older members of the team thought that it was going to be a cake walk. The younger members of the team Ian De Sales la Terriere and Mike Perkins both performed creditably while Hawkey was only brought into the team for the last Test and was palpably not match tight.

The SRA were understandably anxious for revenge and lost no time in inviting South Africa to visit Britain so that only 16 months after the last Test in Johannesburg the South African team arrived in England to play three Test matches. The South African team was similar to that which had beaten Great Britain in South Africa with one important exception. Brian Callaghan who had played first string for South Africa in the first three Tests could not find time to make the trip, his place being taken by an Englishman temporarily living in Rhodesia — David Hodgson. But it was the British team which had a new look and La Terriere who had played first string in two of the Test matches in South Africa played in only the first Test in England — and then at fifth string while Hawkey came into the last two Tests at fourth string. Great Britain started rather shakily only winning the first Test 3-2 but thereafter were completely on top, with both the remaining Tests being won without the loss of a tie. The third Test was played at Edinburgh and was notable for the inclusion in the British team for the first time of Michael Oddy, the best player produced by Scotland for many a year. Oddy was not an original choice, but Nigel Broomfield had to withdraw on account of injury and the inclusion of Oddy was naturally much to the liking of the Scots. What is more, he won his tie against Tony Barnes whose father had been the professional at the Edinburgh Sports Club and where Tony was well remembered.

While the fast Lansdowne courts, where the first Test was played, approximated to the pace of the courts to which the South Africans were accustomed, the slow and colder courts at Cardiff and Edinburgh where the other Tests were played posed problems with which the South Africans were unable to cope.

Why, it may be asked, did the play of the British team in South Africa and the South African team in Britain deteriorate as the tour went on? The answer probably lies in the strain to which members of a touring team are subjected. The almost continuous travelling, living out of a suitcase, too many matches and above all, too much hospitality are all valid reasons which make its difficult for a touring team whether it be at international or club level to give of its best over the period normally covered by a squash tour. It is only natural that a club which is accorded the honour of hosting a visiting team should want to 'push the boat out' as far as the post match entertainment is concerned. Moreover, in Australia and South Africa squash matches start later than they normally do in England and this means that it is well after midnight before the visiting team can get to bed. There are also temptations to be overcome and the locals are keen to show the visitors the town's night life even if it is restricted to visiting the home of a member of the team for a 'nightcap' or tea or coffee. Well meaning excessive hospitality is one of the greatest hazards to touring teams.

It is obviously cheaper to get members of such teams put up in private homes rather than in hotels, but certain members of the Australian teams visiting Britain were not slow to voice their preference for hotels where they felt free to come and go as they pleased, and where they could stay in bed all day if they felt like it. As sponsorship has brought more money into the game, host countries can now generally afford to house visiting international teams in hotels.

Two years later (in 1958) a strong Jesters team toured South Africa and was undefeated. The team consisted of M. J. Perkins (captain), R. M. H. Boddington, N. H. R. A. Broomfield, J. G. A. Lyon and M. A. Oddy. On arrival in Johannesburg M. R. Coulman joined the team. Some indication of the strength of the team may be gauged from the fact that all five of the team which left England had reached the last eight of the Amateur Championship that year. The Jesters just

19

managed to beat the full strength of South Africa. This must surely rank as the strongest club side ever to tour outside England.

Meanwhile stories of the great progress the game was making in Australia were circulating. In 1956 Brian Boys the Australian Amateur Champion spent part of the season in England. He reached the final of the South of England Championship in which he was convincingly beaten by the Egyptian, I. Amin, who also beat him 3-0 in the Amateur Championship. Finally, in 1959 the SRA of Australia endorsed an invitation from the SRA of New South Wales to the SRA in England to send a Great Britain team to tour Australia in the middle of 1959 at a total cost to the SRA of £1,000. Eventually this became a full blown International tour which included three Tests against Australia as well as three against New Zealand (only the last of these latter were played in New Zealand, the first two being played in Australia). The British team of Roy Wilson (captain), Nigel Broomfield, Denis Hughes, Jeremy Lyon and Michael Oddy was the strongest available with only Mike Perkins unable to make the trip. A month's squash in and around Sydney left the team undefeated and in fact in the 25 matches played in Australia only one tie was lost. But if the standard of the opposition was lower than had been expected, the keenness and enthusiasm for the game were unmistakable and several promising players were noted including a young man called Hiscoe. It was also noted that the number of squash courts in New South Wales had in three years increased from 12 to 300. It was obvious that sooner or later some of the Australian players were bound to be good. The team moved on to New Zealand where a further nine matches were played without the loss of a tie. To have played 34 matches and two championships in 58 days was a tremendous physical achievement. It was just as well that much of the opposition was of mediocre quality.

Only three and a half years later Australia sent a team to England and in the only international match with Great Britain, convincingly won 4-1, the same margin by which England was beaten by the tourists. To rub salt into our wounds, Ken Hiscoe, the 'promising player' noted by the British team in Australia, captured the Amateur Championship. Also visiting England at the same time was South Africa. Although beaten 4-1 by England, South Africa put up a tremendous fight against Great Britain only winning in the fifth game of the deciding match. Australia had no difficulty in beating South Africa 4-1.

To finish off the record of matches against Australia, full advantage was taken of the Australian pilgrimage to the British Amateur Championship to play a match between the two countries in both 1964 and 1965, but on each occasion Australia were victorious by three ties to love.

Matches between Great Britain and South Africa were easier to arrange because the distance is less and the fares less than to Australia. In 1965 a four man British side toured Rhodesia and South Africa, playing five three-a-side Tests. A desperately close series saw Great Britain victorious by three Tests to two. But had Dawie Botha been able to capitalise on his one match point against Gerald Massy in the first Test, the result would have been reversed. Once again it was the old story of the touring team being exhausted by the end of the tour but the first three Tests were won and so the loss of the last two did not matter so much. Richard Boddington, who had been a member of the Jesters team in South Africa captained the team with great success. Concurrently with the British team, a Colts (under-23) team toured South Africa. Under the captaincy of David Brazier who later played for Great Britain, the team lost only two matches out of a total of 18.

In 1970 a not very strong British team toured South Africa playing three Test matches, losing them all. Boddington again captained the side but in a non-playing capacity. Squashwise the success of the team was Philip Ayton who although seeded only No 6 won the South African Championship beating in the final Graham MacDonald.

The last series of matches between Great Britain and South Africa was in 1972/3 in England. South Africa was weakened by the last minute inability through illness of Doug Barrow to make the trip. In spite of this, this series was the closest of all encounters between the two countries, South Africa winning the first Test 3-2 and Great Britain the remaining two by a similar margin. The tour was made less pleasant by reason of the anti-apartheid elements in England whose threats of violence and demonstrations caused some of the matches to be played in great secrecy.

POST WAR ADMINISTRATION

When in 1946 steps were taken to revive the SRA it was found necessary to start from scratch. The pre-war honorary secretary W. G. Peasgood who had been on the staff of the RAC, and had been allowed by that indulgent body to devote part of his work time to the work of the SRA, had unfortunately gone blind and was no longer able to work. The secretarial work of the re-formed SRA devolved on Miss Coles, personal assistant to the Secretary of the RAC who had not the time to devote to this work. Captain Palmer-Tomkinson the Chairman, assisted by a small group of pre-war members of the Committee did what they could in their spare time.

An informal meeting of interested parties and of such members of the pre-war Executive Committee as could be contacted was held in May 1946 under the chairmanship of Captain Palmer-Tomkinson. A wide variety of subjects was discussed including the preliminary arrangements for getting the Inter-County Championship going during the 1946/47 season. The decision was made to call a general meeting at which various amendments to the rules of the Association could be formalised. Almost immediately afterwards, a meeting of the Professionals Committee was held under the chairmanship of Colonel W. F. Basset, who was the pre-war Vice-Chairman of the SRA.

The not inconsiderable amount of secretarial work involved in getting the SRA on its feet again soon proved too much for Miss Coles but to the rescue came Mr Duncan Ferguson, a partner in a firm of chartered accountants, one of whose clients was the RAC. Mr Ferguson became nominally the Secretary, with much of the routine work being undertaken by his junior staff. For the first time in the history of the SRA the secretarial offices left the RAC and were moved to Mr Ferguson's office in the City. The rapid growth of the game and the SRA in the post-war years soon posed problems. It became increasingly clear that the growth of the Association was being hampered by the lack of a full time secretary, but the finances of the Association based on pre-war subscription rates certainly did not justify this. In the 1938/39 year the income of the SRA was a mere £260.

The work of the Association was really carried out at meetings of the Executive Committee and much of the time at meetings was wasted by the transaction thereat of purely routine business which could have been settled on his own initiative by a full time secretary, or by a small sub-committee. I finally brought matters to a head by writing a memorandum to the Chairman in which I criticised the existing administration and suggested the appointment of a number of sub-committees whose decisions would be reported to the Executive Committee, which would be left free to deal with matters of policy. Prior to the War, and after the War until 1947 there were only four sub-committees — the Professionals, the Ball, the Championship and Finance. My chief suggestion was the establishment of a General Purposes Committee, but I also advocated sub-committees to deal with the Inter-County Championship, the Rules, Finance, and the Handbook. My proposals were well received by Captain Palmer-Tomkinson who summoned me to dine with him at the Bath Club. Also asked to dinner were Colonel Philip Le Gros and Mr Frank Strawson. The latter, unfortunately, was taken ill and could not be present. The Chairman kept his own supply of port at the Bath Club which did not in any way hinder the progress of business after dinner. The result was that all my proposals were accepted but the Chairman then informed Philip and I that as he was retiring from the Stock Exchange and would thereafter be living in the country, he wished to give up the Chairmanship of the Association. It was known by then that the Vice-Chairman Colonel Bassett was in failing health and also wanted to retire. We were asked who we thought would be a suitable replacement for the Chairman. The claims of Philip Le Gros and Frank Strawson were very evenly balanced and the absence of Frank Strawson relieved one of having to make an embarrassing choice. I suggested Philip Le Gros and so it became. John Ridgers became Vice-Chairman. The position of President, held before the War by the Earl of Kimberley who was killed in the War, had never been filled, so it was natural that Captain Palmer-Tomkinson should succeed to the

Presidency. The only Officer of the Association who had been in office before the War was the Treasurer, Cecil Browning, and he continued in office until 1948. It did not seem at all odd in those friendly days that the accounts of the SRA were audited (of course at no cost!) by the firm in which he was a partner.

There can be no doubt that the efficiency of the SRA was increased by this decentralisation of its administration. I received a generous proportion of the 'portfolios' being appointed Chairman of the Inter-County and the Rules Committees and a member of the General Purposes and Handbook Committees.

The late Wing Commander Jimmy Lawson was Chairman of the Handbook Committee and it was necessary that every effort should be made to get out a new edition of this volume as soon as possible, as the publication had been suspended since the 1938/9 edition, and the Handbook has always been regarded as a valuable piece of window dressing, and a good recruiting counter for individual members of the SRA who received a free copy (they got very little else for their subscription!). The members of the sub-committee were happy to accept their Chairman's offer to do the donkey work once the contents had been decided but it was a shock to discover that three days before the printers deadline for copy, pressure of work had made it impossible for the Chairman to do the work. However somehow a 67 page Handbook was assembled in one week-end and honour was saved. Every year since, the Handbook has been published, usually on October 1st. In 1974 however editorial and production difficulties resulted in publication date being postponed until February 1975. In size the Handbook has grown rapidly and the 1976/7 edition ran to 432 pages.

Slowly the newly re-formed Association began to feel its feet. By the middle of 1947, reconstruction was almost complete. The Amateur Championship had been revived in December 1946 and the Inter County Championship was held with 15 counties competing. The Executive and sub-committees were all working hard at reconstruction and all this placed a great and ever increasing strain on the office staff of Mr Ferguson's firm. For a time the pressure was relieved by a decision that sub-committees were to make their own arrangements for typing, copying and distributing their minutes. It became obvious that only the creation of the SRA's own secretarial and headquarters would satisfactorily solve the problem. Finally the General Meeting held in June 1948 authorised the Executive Committee to institute the appointment of a full time secretary. At that time the SRA could not afford to pay the secretary a living wage (a state of affairs which existed up to 1972!). But Mr H. E. Hayman, who had done a fine job as Hon Secretary of the Surrey SRA offered to take on the job at a salary of £350 a year, and in September 1948 the offer was accepted. But where to work? Again the Association was lucky and an offer was received, and gratefully accepted — from the Federation of British

Manufacturers of Sports and Games of a tiny room in their office just off the Haymarket in central London, at an annual rental of £100. The room was just large enough for one desk but a small table was also squeezed in which acted as a desk for those weeks at the height of the season when an assistant secretary was appointed to help the secretary with the Championships. The first of these annual appointments was Peter Doggart, who was also the first of a long line of top class young players. Between 1955 and 1968 when the first full time assistant secretary was appointed, of the 13 assistant secretaries seven subsequently played for their country. They came to the SRA office because it offered them temporary employment at the game they loved and were given the opportunity of improving their squash by an indulgent secretary who gave them time off if necessary for matches. Their knowledge of the game and its leading figures was useful when it came to organising the Amateur and Open Championships.

The cramped conditions at the Haymarket were endured for 13 years until their landlords, the FBMSG moved to other premises. Again the SRA was lucky in being given in February 1961 a somewhat larger room in the London showrooms of H. J. Gray and Sons, and this lasted until November 1963 when a number of minor sports were encouraged by the Government to take up some surplus accommodation in new offices in Park Crescent, Regents Park, which were mainly to be used as the Headquarters of the Central Council of Physical Recreation. The SRA was allotted one and a half rooms (the half shared with the Hockey Association) and subsequently two rooms, which, if not large, were very much in excess of anything which had been enjoyed before. Finally early in 1974 the Sports Council with its satelite associations moved into yet more luxurious accommodation in the building of the Independent Broadcasting Authority in Knightsbridge. Here the SRA has the use of four large and one small rooms — and needed every inch of the space.

But to return to the late forties, Henry Hayman remained with the SRA for seven years. There can be no doubt that employment of a full time secretary contributed very materially to the post-war growth of the SRA. During Hayman's seven year tenure of office the number of individual members of the Association rose from 153 to 749. The SRA relied very heavily on individual subscriptions which during all this period remained at one guinea. The benefits of membership were meagre but one of the first was the provision of a tie limited to individual members. In those days of post war shortages it was almost impossible to get new designs woven but Messrs Lewins of Jermyn Street came to the rescue of the Association by producing a tie which had been ordered by some university club in 1939. The outbreak of the War had killed the club but the last of the tie had survived. Stripes of black, orange and mauve could hardly be said to have much connection with either squash rackets or the Association, but it was either this or nothing and for four years this was the official SRA tie until the present tie consisting of crossed rackets with the Lancastrian crown in between the racket heads. This emblem of the SRA does not appear to have been adopted by the SRA until after the War. The late Mr J. B. Rosher, who was Legal Adviser to the SRA, at one time raised the awkward question of whether the Association was entitled to use the Royal rose as its emblem. The Highest Quarters were consulted and while it transpired that Mr Rosher's doubts were justified the Association was informed that a blind and benevolent eye would be turned on this act of treason or whatever.

Undoubtedly the tie was the best recruiting counter for membership of the SRA and it was particularly popular with the juniors.

Individual membership was instituted in 1931 and in the first year a modest 38 members were enrolled. Little effort seems to have been made to increase this number and in the last year before the War it had risen to only 62. In the first season after the War there were 36 individual members, but with the appointment of a full time secretary the numbers rose rapidly and when Henry Hayman left in 1955 it had reached 749. In the decade ending in 1960 there was a net increase of 670 members and in the next decade ending in 1970 the net increase had risen to about 1,300. Yet it was only in the last four years of this decade that most of this increase occurred. As time went by, the number of deaths, resignations and removals for non-payment steadily increased, so that the net figure does not do justice to the number of new members who poured in. The number of individual members were spurred on by a decision to make membership compulsory for all those who attended the SRA Coaching Courses, and in addition, home players wanting to compete in the Amateur and Amateur Veterans Championships had to be Individual Members.

The decision to raise the individual members subscription from £1.05 to £2.00 in 1971 caused chaos. Apart from a large and expected number of resignations, hundreds of members who paid their subscriptions by bankers order did not take the trouble to sign a new order and continued to pay at the old sum. It was some years before matters were sorted out and a large number of members were allowed to continue at the old rate but with reduced benefits. In recent years the individual members subscription has suffered from inflation and was increased to £3.50 in 1977 and to £5.00 in 1978.

In 1949 a Life membership was instituted and was cheap at ten guineas. This was increased to £25 in 1971. This figure was further increased to £35 in 1977 and to £75 in 1978.

Before the War individual members of county associations were automatically individual members of the SRA. County Membership was at the discretion of the county association concerned and was usually only 10/- or even 7/6d. County associations were supposed to pay 5/- per annum of this sum to the SRA. Some did — others did not. It was obviously absurd that some members, because they were members of their county association to which they paid perhaps ten shillings, should get all the benefits of individual membership for which others had to pay a guinea. It was therefore decided by the SRA that each county association should pay to the SRA annually a guinea for each of its individual members. As may be expected, there were violent objections raised by the counties, and peace was not restored until it was decided that members of county associations should not automatically also become individual members of the SRA.

The revenue from individual membership was, in the early days after War, the life blood of the SRA. The difficulty was to persuade players that a governing body was necessary and cost an increasing amount to run. The benefits of individual membership — of which the main ones were the right to wear the SRA tie, the right to obtain tickets for the SRA Championships before they became available to the general public, and a free copy of the SRA Handbook — were not of great value and most members who joined looked upon their subscription as a charitable donation to the SRA. The tie was probably the best recruiting counter — the SRA Handbook could be bought by the public for only five shillings.

A junior membership for those under 19 was instituted in 1949 and cost the young player only five shillings. The benefits of junior membership were more substantial, for in addition to the right to wear the tie, and to receive a free Handbook, the young member could purchase tickets for all but the last three rounds of the SRA Championships at half price. Junior membership was an immediate success and rose from 31 in 1949 to 202 in 1952. Foolishly the SRA thought that they were giving too much away for too little and decided to double the subscription. The effect was catastrophic and the numbers were halved. However the position was saved by increasing the age limit from 19 to 21 and once again the numbers soared. The number of schools playing the game either on their own or on borrowed courts increased in the early sixties and this also helped to swell the junior interest in squash and hence the number of junior members. The peak period was 1962-1963 when there were well over 300 junior members on the books. Again the SRA thought that they were giving too much away and in 1966 dealt a double blow by increasing the subscription to seven shillings and sixpence and decreasing the age limit to 19. By 1967 the number of junior members was halved and for some reason continued to decline. In 1970 the subscription was raised to ten shillings.

While there is no doubt that the junior members were getting a great deal for their money — the Handbook at this time was sold to the public at ten shillings — and that junior membership was heavily subsidised, it was the old story of a 'sprat to catch a mackerel'. Every junior member on reaching the age limit was invited to transfer to individual membership and a fairly high proportion who had become accustomed to receiving, not only the Handbook, but all the other handouts including copies of the draw for the Amateur and Open Championships, thought it worthwhile to continue.

Why then, in an era of rapid expansion of the game and of the building of courts at an increasing number of schools, is junior membership at such a low ebb? Probably the reason lies in that rapid expansion of the game which put such an intolerable strain on the headquarters administration of the SRA that there was not time to give to junior recruiting campaigns. Moreover the financial return from junior membership became mere 'chicken feed' as the Sports Council continued to pour ever increasing grants to the administration of the game.

By the early seventies, increasing Government grants and other sources of revenue resulted in members subscriptions playing a less important part in the finances of the SRA. The Headquarters staff were too busy on possibly more important matters to get among the juniors and mount recruiting drives.

CHAPTER III

INTERNATIONAL ADMINISTRATION

*T*HE HISTORY of international squash in the early sixties is strangely reminiscent of the break up of the British Empire. The rapid increase in the standard of Australian and South African squash played a prominent part in formulating a desire by Australia to wrest the unofficial world titles from the British Championships, both Open and Amateur. Once Australia had shown themselves capable of beating Great Britain they began to hanker after holding a world championship in their own country. They argued, not without reason, that it was unfair on them to have to send their players half way round the world every year to win the British Amateur Championship, considered and even acknowledged as the World Amateur Championship, even if not so titled.

In the 1962-63 season amateur representative teams from Australia and South Africa visited England and the opportunity was taken to hold a meeting at which all three countries were represented. As usual the main talking point was money or the lack of it. Great Britain stated that it was impossible for the SRA either to receive or visit Australia or South Africa at intervals of less than three years. South Africa suggested that there should be a central body to organise overseas tours with a central fund out of which all tour expenses should be paid. In order to reduce travelling costs it was decided that future overseas teams between the countries represented at the meeting should be limited to three (plus a reserve). Although this proposal was brought into effect in the first International Championship in 1967, the British team which was to visit South Africa in 1965 consisted of six players.

The Australian delegates suggested that as soon as practicable, teams from South Africa and Great Britain should visit Australia at the same time and that in that year the Australian Amateur Championship should be described as the World Championship. This attempt to capture the title from Great Britain was viewed with understandable suspicion by the other two countries and the proposal was defeated.

Finally the conference approved the setting up of a co-ordinating body to discuss international matters which should meet as occasion demanded.

One interesting point was made at the conference when the captain of the Australian team stated that 40% of the cost of the fares of his team to England had been met by commercial concerns — one of the earliest references to sponsorship.

A year later Major Mourad, the manager of the Egyptian team touring England in an interview in 'The Times' suggested the formation of an international federation to promote an annual championship in all the leading squash playing countries in turn. Thus were fired the first shots in a struggle for world power in squash, and shortly afterwards the President of the Australian SRA delivered a broadside in the form of a letter to the national associations of Great Britain (the SRA), Egypt, Pakistan, South Africa, New Zealand and the USA in which agreement or otherwise was invited to six suggestions which embodied the formation of an international federation. There was a good deal of activity going on behind the scenes, and the Secretary of the SRA visited South Africa and Egypt for talks. Australia was keen to have a world championship moving round the countries to which their letter had been addressed, but the inclusion of South Africa in this programme raised difficulties. Certain countries would not permit their players to play in that country but it was suggested that this could be got over by holding the championship, when South Africa's turn came round, in Rhodesia which was affiliated to, and part of, the SRA of Southern Africa. This ingenious way out was unfortunately destroyed by Rhodesia's declaration of independence.

Yet there was an undoubted desire to form some sort of body which, international in character, would take over from the SRA the administration of world squash, and the SRA called a conference in January 1966 of representatives of those countries to which the Australian President's letter of the previous year had been addressed, but without the USA and with the addition of India.

The case of the USA and Canada raised peculiar difficulties. The differences between the British and American games was such that it was considered that international competition between the countries playing the two games was impracticable. Nevertheless, it was unthinkable that these two great squash playing countries should be just ignored, and they were invited to send their representatives to the conference as observers. The addition of India was interesting. The British had introduced squash to India as indeed to most countries, and the large number of Army and civilian personnel stationed in India had contributed to a considerable number of courts being built there during the first half of the twentieth century. But the end of the British Raj and the splitting of the country into India and Pakistan undoubtedly diminished the standard as well as the amount of squash played in India. There was probably less squash played in India than in the other countries invited to the conference. Yet to include Pakistan and exclude India would have been a diplomatic gaffe of the first order. While these considerations had not presumably been in the mind of the Australian President when he wrote his letter suggesting an international federation, there is no doubt that India had a good claim to be represented at the Conference and their delegate, Mr Ahmed Peermahomed, who later became their official representative on the Federation, attended every meeting of that body.

The Conference had no difficulty in agreeing to form an international federation, and went so far as to adopt a Constitution. The hope was expressed that an international team series should be held as near annually as possible commencing in Australia in 1967. This goal proved over optimistic, and with the series alternating as far as possible between the Northern and Southern Hemispheres and held in the countries designated in the Constitution as Founder Members, difficulties were created by the differences between the squash seasons in the two hemispheres.

There were seven nations represented at the meeting — Australia, Great Britain, India, New Zealand, Pakistan, South Africa and the United Arab Republic (Egypt). These were designated Founder Members and it was agreed that only Full and Founder Members should be allowed to participate in the International Amateur Championships as they were to be called.

There was little difficulty in agreeing that the first Amateur International Championships should be played in Australia. The team event was generally regarded as the more important of the two competitons but it was obvious that there should be more than the one event and accordingly an individual event was added to which it was hoped that the host country would add a plate event.

The venue of the next championships was not so easy. Obviously it would be inexpedient to hold them in England when there were other countries in the Northern Hemisphere ready and indeed eager to stage them. Eventually it was decided that they should go to Egypt in November 1968, and after that either to Great Britain or to Pakistan.

When the meeting turned to finding trophies for the events there was quite a rush of countries wishing to present them. It was felt that it would be invidious to choose between the offers and it was finally decided that the trophies should be presented by the Federation, but one made in India and the other in Pakistan. Current currency restrictions made it difficult for these two countries to remit their subscriptions to the headquarters of the Federation in England and it was therefore agreed that as it had been laid down that the price of each trophy should not exceed £100, which happened to be the amount of the subscription, these two countries would present their trophies in lieu of their first years subscriptions.

The outbreak of hostilities in the Middle East destroyed any hope of Egypt being able to host the Championships in the 1968/9 season and Pakistan agreed to stand down to enable the Championships to be held in England during that season. This was the last occasion when South Africa would be able to compete alongside Pakistan, India or Egypt, and indeed, if the venue had been Pakistan, South Africa would not have been permitted to play in that country.

The Constitution adopted by the newly formed Federation laid down that one of its objects should be "to uphold the rules of the game of Squash Rackets adopted by the Federation". This meant that neither the USA nor Canada could be elected as Members as they could not subscribe to the British code of rules.

This ban was partially lifted when those who could not subscribe to British Rules were made eligible for Associate Membership and which gave them the right to attend and address meetings, but not to vote. So the USA and Canada were elected to Associate Membership in 1968, and finally when the Constitution was again changed in 1969 to Full Membership. At the 1971 meeting of the Federation held in New Zealand it was decided, on the proposition of Australia, that Canada and the USA should be added to the list of Founder Members on the grounds that they would have become Founder Members had they been eligible. Although the validity of this decision is open to question, there was no doubt that it was the wish of the Members.

The presence of South Africa as a Founder Member has led to difficulties and controversy and only the diplomatic skill of certain individuals has saved the Federation from disintegration on the issue of apartheid. During the early years of the Federation the attitude of the Afro-Asian nations against South Africa and its apartheid policy was gradually hardening. After the 1969 Championships in England in which South Africa, Egypt and Pakistan (but not India) all competed against each other quite happily, it was said that the manager of one of the teams was censored on returning home for allowing his team to play South Africa. At the General Meeting of the Federation held at the same time as the 1969 Championships, Egypt, India and Pakistan were unable to give an assurance that, should they host the Championships, their Governments would be able or willing to permit the entry of a South African team. Under the Rules governing Amateur International Championships, the host nation is required to issue invitations to all Full Members. This caused the temporary withdrawal of Pakistan as a potential host nation for the 1971 Championships which it was therefore decided should be held in New Zealand. But worse was to come when in 1970 a resolution was received from Pakistan that South Africa should be excluded from the Federation. This necessitated the calling of an Extraordinary General Meeting which was held in London in July 1970. The Pakistan representative, Cdr A. Rashid stated that he was doing this solely in the interests of Pakistan squash, in that his Government had supported the resolution of the Committee of Human Rights and banned all Pakistani teams from taking part in competitions in which South African teams figured. Thus only by the exclusion of South Africa would it be possible for Pakistan to take part in future International Championships. The South African delegate replied that his country would be in a position to welcome members of all nations, should the Championships be held in South Africa but offered not to send a team to New Zealand in order to ensure Pakistan's competition in 1971. Eventually Pakistan was persuaded to withdraw its resolution on South Africa undertaking not to send a team to New Zealand. The policy of the Federation has always been to play for time in the expectation that eventually there would be a relaxation of the sporting bans between South Africa and the anti-apartheid nations.

The venue of the 1973 Championships caused further difficulty at the meeting held in New Zealand at the time of the 1971 International Championships, and eventually it was decided that Pakistan should be the host nation, but only on condition that they should be in a position to give an assurance by early in 1972 that an invitation could be sent to every member nation. This seemed so unlikely even then that an alternative had to be agreed. Thus it came about that South Africa was chosen as the alternative on the understanding that a letter from the South African Government would be received stating that nations of all colours and creeds would be made welcome. As was expected, Pakistan was unable to give the necessary assurances for not only would her Government refuse to admit South Africa, but the onset of the war between Pakistan and India made it unlikely that an Indian team would be persona grata in Pakistan. Thus it came about that South Africa was the unlikely venue chosen. Her delegate at the New Zealand meeting undertook to organise a tournament in South Africa in July 1972 to which invitations to send players to take part in would be sent to the national associations of Egypt, India and Pakistan. This duly took place but the only national of these countries who competed was Sharif Khan, who came from Canada where he was a resident professional.

The 1973 Championships were held in South Africa but in spite of the assurance provided by the South African Government that players of all colours would be made welcome, no teams from Egypt, India or Pakistan competed. To make matters worse, only a month before the commencement of the Championships, Canada withdrew, bowing to pressure from the Canadian Government who threatened to cut off financial aid to the Canadian SRA if the team played in South Africa.

Meetings of the ISRF are normally held during the International Championships and it became apparent that the Governments of the three coloured member nations would not permit their delegates to go to South Africa. A way round this difficulty was found by holding the meeting in the small independent state of Swaziland which is almost entirely surrounded by South Africa and only a short flight away from Johannesburg. At this meeting the shadow of apartheid was again looming over the meeting when the venue of the next Championships came up for discussion. It had been agreed at the New Zealand meeting in 1971 that the 1975 Championships should go to Canada, but the Canadian delegate was unhappy about the actual date being under the impression that 1975 meant the 1975/6 season with April-May 1976 as the likely date. Canada wanted more time to erect international sized courts, but there was also the difficulty of whether the Canadian Government would permit a South African team to play in view of their attitude to the Canadians playing in South Africa — and even if the South Africans were admitted it was doubtful if the coloured teams would have been permitted by their Governments to play against South Africa. Eventually Canada offered to step down to permit either Egypt or Pakistan to host the Championships on the understanding that Canada should have the next Championships after that. This was incorporated in a resolution from the chair which was carried. Egypt was given until 31st January 1974 to accept the Championship, failing which they should go to Pakistan. If neither of these countries were able to accept, the Championships were to go to Canada but that these were not to be played until 1976. In the event, Egypt so recently at war with Israel withdrew, and Pakistan accepted. It was tacitly agreed that South Africa would not send a team to Pakistan.

But now Pakistan got into difficulties and had to withdraw, and because Canada was hosting the Olympic Games in 1976 it fell to England to fill the gap in that year, with Canada's turn coming up in 1977. This delay was all to the good as far as Canada was concerned for it gave her more time to build International courts and for their players to become accustomed to the International and soft ball game. At the ISRF meeting held in the middle of the 1977 International Amateur Championships much time was taken up over the venue of the following Championships with Egypt eager to hold them. Finally they were allocated to Egypt providing that country could give satisfactory assurances over the venues, the facilities and the budget. These were not forthcoming by the date laid down and Australia, being in a position to give these assurances, were finally awarded the Championships for 1979 (October) with the 1981 Championships going to Sweden.

Although it has been the practice to hold the General Meetings of the ISRF during the Championships the question of the venue of the 1977 meeting caused further trouble. Although not competing South Africa wanted to be present at the General Meeting. However this meeting was due to take place only a few months before the 1978 Commonwealth Games were scheduled to be held in Canada. The Canadians were fearful that the Afro-Asian countries due to take part in the Games might take exception if they learned that South Africans had attended the ISRF meeting in Canada. It was accordingly arranged that the meeting should be held in Buffalo, just over the Canadian border in the USA and only 100 miles from Toronto when the Individual Event of the Championships were just beginning. The Americans proved generous hosts and yet another hurdle was jumped in the nick of time.

At every meeting of the Federation an immense amount of time has been taken up with discussions on the South African difficulty, but there has been another problem which has had to be faced at these meetings — the American game.

Squash in America has been growing, if not at quite the rate of expansion of England, yet at a pace and on a scale which entitled at any rate the USA to be regarded as one of the leading squash nations of the world. When the original constitution of the ISRF was passed, one of the objects laid down was to uphold the rules adopted by the Federation and at the inaugural meeting it had been agreed that the rules of the game adopted by the Federation should be those laid down in the then current edition of the SRA Handbook, i.e. the British rules.

This ruled out American and Canadian membership of the Federation. Neither of these countries wanted to be left out in the cold, and moreover, the Federation could not be said to be truly international if such leading centres of the game were excluded from membership. The position was finally resolved at the 1969 meeting when a further amendment of the Consitution was passed which was directly aimed at facilitating American and Canadian entries as Full Members. This was achieved by stating that the playing rules of the Federation should be those of the SRA of Great Britain except that on the continent of North America where they should be those of the USSRA.

As a result of this the USA and Canada were immediately elected Full Members and have since always played an important part in the activities of the Federation. At the same meeting an attempt was made to investigate the possibilities of integrating the two games by appointing a committee to investigate this, but the proposal was defeated. What was agreed however was that all Federation Championships wherever held should be governed by British rules of play.

Since 1946 there have been sporadic efforts to bring the two games together. In the 1954-55 season the SRA asked all clubs to experiment with American scoring, but the clubs by a large majority reported that their members, having tried it, did not like it.

The next step was a scheme devised by Mr Stewart Brauns, at that time President of the USSRA. He presented this at the 1971 meeting of the Federation. His proposals were to create a game for international play level. He accepted the international ball — the Australian Yellow Dot, but in return wanted American type scoring retained as well as American court markings, including the white painted floor. The Members of the Federation were asked to carry out trials and to report back. Apart from the North American Members who were understandably in favour, no Member reported that they thought the scheme a good one and the compromise game was interred with some speed at the following 1973 meeting of the Federation.

It would seem that there is now little chance of bringing the two games together. There are far too many courts in existence to make remotely possible any conversion to a different size by either party. Over the years it seems that American scoring is not popular outside North America, although it is used to a certain extent in club handicap events in England.

It is always necessary to put in a lot of practice at the other game before the start of a tour. The general impression is that it is easier for the British to take up the American game than vice versa and this is strikingly borne out by the results. Gerald Robarts, a member of the British team which toured America in 1924 won the US Amateur Championship in that year while in 1927, the British touring team were permitted to take part in the Lapham Trophy matches normally played annually between the US and Canada — and won the Trophy. Miss Janet Morgan won the US Womens Championship in 1955. But American teams and individuals have never been successful in this country and no American has ever won a tie in England in either mens or womens international matches.

In 1971 Canada sent a team to compete in the International Championships in New Zealand and in 1973 the USA sent a team to play in South Africa, but neither of these sides made any impression on the teams used to playing the international game.

In 1976 both the USA and Canada sent teams to England. Largely by virtue of the fact that the International game has made more strides in Canada — partly with an eye to the hosting of the Championships there in 1977 — the Canadian players adapted themselves more readily to the International game and defeated the USA 2-1.

Early General Meetings of the Federation were completed in one day, but the complexity of many of the issues raised led to longer and longer meetings. In 1971 the meeting in Hamilton, New Zealand lasted until nearly lunchtime on the second day; in 1973 the meeting could well have occupied two whole days, but the delegates were booked to return to Johannesburg on the afternoon flight and there was a scramble to get through the later items of the agenda in order to catch the plane. The 1975 meeting in London spread over to the afternoon of the second day while, in the following year it was only by hard slogging that the meeting ended at after 7.00 p.m. on the third day. The Minutes of this last meeting ran to 40 foolscap pages. On the other hand, the Buffalo meeting in 1977 was completed inside two days.

Apart from the position of South Africa, particularly as to how this affected the venue of the Championships, the meetings discussed changes in the Rules of the game and the Rules Governing International Championships. Another subject which took up countless hours over the years was the proposal to abolish amateur status. This had first been proposed by Great Britain at the 1970 meeting. The opposition to the proposal was led by Australia and, although heavily defeated, Great Britain came up with the same prosposal and with the same result in 1971. In 1973 and 1975 Sweden took up the fight, and also failed decisively. This subject was closely linked with the difficulties of obtaining an agreed definition of amateur status which would be enforceable by all Members. Criteria for Membership was another subject discussion on which stretched through several meetings.

But perhaps more time was spent in debating a new Constitution than on any other subject. The original Constitution conceived somewhat hastily in 1966-67 had stood up remarkably well to the expansion of the game as well as of the Federation. But in 1971 the USA proposed that an ad hoc committee be set up "to study thoroughly the Constitution in its entirety and submit recommended changes, additions or deletions". This was asking for it, and the meeting gratefully accepted the offer of the USA to carry out the task. In the event Mr S. Brauns, the USA Representative became Chairman of the Constitution sub-committee and a long dialogue ensued between the sub-committee and the Federation Officers before the final draft was considered at length by the 1973 Federation meeting. But Mr Howard Bilbrough, Vice-Chairman of the SRA of Southern Africa and himself a noted lawyer submitted a memorandum setting forth a number of points of drafting and of principle on which he differed from the draft new Constitution. Finally it was agreed that Mr Bilbrough should put forward a new draft and this was finally approved at the 1975 meeting.

All this was, of course, in addition to routine matters such as finance, election of Officers and a multitude of resolutions on a wide variety of squash subjects submitted by Members.

The 1975 meeting, which was held in London because there were no International Championships held in that year was the end of an era as far as the Federation was concerned. Mr P. J. Phillips, an Englishman had been elected Chairman at the first meeting in 1966 and had been re-elected at every subsequent meeting. In the absence of an executive committee the routine work of the Federation fell on the Chairman and the other Officers, who found it necessary to meet on average once a month. It was obvious that the Officers must be resident in the same country if there were to be regular attenders at these meetings. By 1975 Mr Phillips re-election was barred by the Constitution. His successor was Mr Murray Day, the New Zealand representative and in consequence the Headquarters of the Federation moved to New Zealand, and the Vice-Chairman, Treasurer and Secretary were all resident there. Under the new Constitution a Fifth Officer had to be elected and this turned out to be Mr R. Villafranca, the Mexican representative. This experiment was not altogether successful for distances involved precluded the Fifth Officer from attending any Officers meetings, and the position was abolished at the 1977 meeting.

The moving of the Headquarters of the Federation to the other end of the world coupled with a complete change of Officers had not such a profound effect on the Federation as some had foreseen. While there had been some understandable desire for a change of management after so many years the new Officers found that many of the members were as loathe to play their part and co-operate in the world wide administration of the game as had been the case under the old regime.

There was one aspect however in which welcome progress was made. The Federation from its inception had been limited to the game as played by amateurs. At the 1973 meeting Australia had put forward a resolution calling for the holding of a World Open Championship to include professionals. Time precluded a full discussion of the proposal and the Officers were instructed to investigate the possibilities and report back to the Members. They subsequently came to the conclusion that the congestion of the world fixture list plus the expense of putting on such a prestigious event was such that it was doubtful if this would turn out to be a feasible proposition. They proposed that the world title should be given to the Open Championships of Great Britain and Australia consecutively for a trial period, starting with the British Open in January 1976, followed by the Australian Open in August 1977. This was approved by the Members and the Federation thereby became officially involved with playing professionals. This followed closely on the formation of the International Squash Players Association (ISPA). Although only formed early in 1974 the playing professionals have lost no time in stating their aims and taking action in support of them. It is worth quoting these aims, as set forth to the ISRF: "to co-ordinate as a professional players' body and to protect that body's interests on an international basis; to liaise and work with all the governing bodies, tournament organisations, and sponsors to further safeguard the future development of competitive professional squash throughout the world".

ISPA, in the administration of which Jonah Barrington, Geoff Hunt and Ken Hiscoe played important roles, forced the governing bodies of the world to agree to its schedules of major tournaments which were arranged so that the leading professionals would visit the main squash countries of the world at such seasons of the year as suited them forcing the national associations to hold their open and professional tournaments at such times as suited ISPA. This body also quickly decided that the World Open Championship should be divorced from the Open Championships of Great Britain and Australia, and a successful first World Open was held in October 1977 in Australia with sponsorship of A40,000 dollars making it at that time the richest squash tournament in the world. Encouraged by this success ISPA announced that the next World Open would be held in England in the early autumn of 1978 but were unable to find a sponsor and the event had to be abandoned.

At the end of the first ten years it is perhaps pertinent to take stock and ask if the ISRF has achieved its objects. Taking into account the vast and world wide increase in the game in recent years, is the membership disappointing? 14 Full Members and seven Associate Members. It is known that the game is played in over 50 countries but many of these have not got national associations, a pre requisite for membership of the Federation. It is the small number of associate members which gives cause for concern. Do they get valued for their annual subscription which may be as low as £10? Those who will not join point out that until they become Full Members they have no vote (but they can attend and speak at meetings) and they therefore feel that they can play little part in the government of the game. In recent years the squash countries of Europe have formed their own federation which 20 of them have already joined. Membership here is not restricted to countries which have national associations. Most members of the European Federation can afford to send five players to the annual championships held in different countries of Western Europe whereas Associate Members were not originally entitled to enter teams in the International Amateur Championships which are held anywhere in the world, so that if they could enter teams the cost of transporting them would be prohibitive to small nations whose governments are either unable or unwilling to contribute to the transportation costs involved.

Yet all sports must have a world governing body to make the rules of the game and to decide the many problems which beset a growing game. The International Federation's argument is that countries should join as Associate or Provisional Members in the hope and expectation that the game in those countries will expand until those members are in a position to apply for promotion to Full or Associate Membership with its enlarged privileges and responsibilities.

There are many parts of the world where squash is virtually unknown except to a small number of British expatriots. The numerous countries of South America are a case in point. There are clubs in Argentina, Brazil and Peru — generally only one club in each of these countries but there has been little sign of growth. Optimists will point to the miracle of squash in Mexico where the number of courts rose from a dozen to 2,000 in the space of a few years. But would this tremendous expansion have taken place if Mexico's borders had not been contiguous to the USA?

Squash is not a game which can be played anywhere at the drop of a hat. A court has to be constructed, often at considerable cost. But everything has to start somewhere and national growth is more likely to flourish as the game obtains better and world wide publicity. Your Barringtons and your Hunts travelling round the world do an immense service to the game when they stop off at places like Manila and play exhibitions. But there must be a follow-up to these recruiting visits. The danger is that the nations will watch the masters perform with admiration for their speed and skill, but will shudder at the thought of trying to imitate them. "Too tiring", they will say, particularly in the tropics. Best left to "mad dogs and Englishmen". In the days when the Squash Rackets Association in England was the world wide de facto governing body of squash the majority of clubs in countries where there was no national association became affiliated to the SRA. It did not cost much (until the last few years only £1) and the handouts kept them acquainted with any changes in the rules of the game and the annual Handbook told them what was going on.

Doubts had been expressed in the mid-seventies whether the ISRF adequately catered for the small nations with little resources either to pay the high rates of subscription or to send teams overseas to compete in the International Championships. As a result, the Buffalo meeting introduced a third category of membership, to be called Provisional designed to attract clubs and bodies in countries which did not possess national associations, and paying only a nominal subscription, and possessing no voting rights, but this received only a modest response. During 1978 however four new Associate Members were elected. Associate Membership had been made more attractive by a resolution carried at the Buffalo meeting permitting Associate Members to participate in the Team Event of the Championships.

It can be argued that the ISRF has not expanded at the same rate as the game itself. The reasons are economic rather than political. The younger squash playing countries have at best financially weak national associations whose financial resources are fully committed to aiding the internal expansion of the game. The lack of gate money is a perpetual drawback to the growth of national associations and squash is at best a participant rather than a spectator sport.

This invariably affects the finances of the world governing body which cannot afford even a paid secretariat. A high — some say too high — proportion of its revenue is spent on sending its officers to distant part of the world 'showing the flag' and hoping to obtain thereby new members — and hence additional revenue — for the ISRF. These are not paid officials but give willingly of their time in the interests of the game and of the Federation.

MICHAEL ODDY — Scotland's best ever player.

CHAPTER IV

HOME COUNTRIES AND OVERSEAS

SCOTLAND

*S*QUASH IN Scotland started in Aberdeen and Glasgow where clubs were in existence before the 1939 War. Also, before 1939 in Edinburgh, the Watsonians and the Edinburgh Academicals owned squash courts as a sideline to their other sporting activities (mostly Rugby Football). In addition, clubs existed at Galashiels and Brechin, and there were a fair number of private courts, the owners of which were generous in letting devotees of the game play in them. In particular, there was a court in Edinburgh owned by T. J. Carlyle Gifford and R. G. Simpson which the owners gave to Edinburgh University after the War.

1936 was the most important date in Scottish squash, for in that year the Edinburgh Sports Club was opened and the Scottish SRA was formed. It was in 1936 also that the first Scottish Amateur Championship was played and won by I. A. Crabbie. This was, however, an unofficial event and it was in 1937 that the newly formed SSRA organised the first official Amateur Championship which was won by W. B. Scott, who probably holds the record for being the heaviest player to win a national championship. The Edinburgh Sports Club at Belford Place rapidly became the centre of squash in Scotland. Starting with three courts, such was the success of the venture that only two years later two more singles courts and a doubles court were added. The Championship court had what was for many years the largest gallery in the United Kingdom. The club now has seven courts in addition to the doubles court, which since the War has been the only one in existence in the UK.

The first international match played by Scotland was against Ireland in February 1938, and won by Scotland 4-1. The only Irish success was at first string where George McVeagh beat W. B. Scott. Less than a month later, any large ideas which the Scots may have entertained as a result of this success were rudely shattered when they tackled England in London. The match, consisting of five singles and two doubles ties was played at St Johns Wood Club which had a doubles court, and the doubles provided Scotland with its sole success when the top Scottish players, R. D. McKelvie and W. B. Scott beat E. Snell and C. L. Stubbs in five games. McKelvie and Scott were probably the best doubles pair in the United Kingdom, and although representing Scotland, played most of their squash in London. In the following year, in the same match, the Scots again triumphed in the doubles winning this time both ties. But a win in the singles eluded them. The matches in Scotland were always played at the Edinburgh Sports Club but doubles matches have been excluded since the War, probably because there were no doubles courts in England. The Scots, not without reason, always gave themselves a chance of victory when the match was played in the comparatively cold courts at Edinburgh, and they were certainly unable to come to terms with the hot courts at the RAC in London where the matches were usually played in England.

The Scots very nearly succeeded in winning the match in 1960. M. A. Oddy and O. L. Balfour won the two top strings for Scotland against J. G. A. Lyon and J. M. G. Tildesley. The latter moved up to second string owing to Richard Boddington having eaten a bad pork pie before entraining for Edinburgh, with disastrous results. Boddington was in no fit state to play but England had no reserve, and so he staggered onto court against the Scottish fifth string, Claude Brownlow, who had merely to keep the ball in play to draw the last reserves of strength out of his weakened opponent. But through inexperience Brownlow tried for winners and hit down repeatedly thereby giving the match to his astonished opponent.

But in 1964 Scotland achieved its ambition and beat England 3-2 in Edinburgh, all depending on the last tie between the third strings G. R. Chisholm (Scotland) and J. F. Skinner (England). This is the only occasion on which Scotland has won and the scores of this match are worth setting out in full:

M. A. Oddy (S) beat R. M. H. Boddington 9-4, 10-8, 9-7.

O. L. Balfour (S) beat J. G. A. Lyon 9-5, 9-3, 5-9, 3-9, 9-5.

G. R. Chisholm (S) beat J. F. Skinner 6-9, 7-9, 9-6, 10-8, 9-1.

R. D. Montgomerie (S) lost to P. G. Kirton 7-9, 7-9, 2-9.

I. C. de Sales la Terriere (S) lost to T. D. Gathercole 8-10, 4-9, 6-9.

Apart from England, Scotland has the best record among the Home Countries. Ireland has only won a handful of matches, but against

Wales, Scotland has a slight advantage.

Over the years, Scotland's greatest player has been Michael Oddy, who twice won the British Amateur Championship, and in addition won the Championships of Australia, New Zealand and South Africa. But Oddy played most of his squash in London. The greatest stroke player so far produced by Scotland is undoubtedly Oliver Balfour, who won the Scottish Amateur three times. He was seldom seen in England, but there are many who think that had he had the opportunity of continuous competitive play down South he would have had a more impressive record. Mention should also be made of the Rev D. W. D. Shaw, whose record is little inferior to that of Olly Balfour. If Bill Shaw's shots were not as spectacular as Balfour's, they were more elegant and were played by one of the greatest 'gentlemen' the game has produced — and that not only in Scotland.

In the pre-Oddy/Balfour era the best player was Paul Harding-Edgar who represented Scotland on 20 occasions. He first played for his country in 1938 and made his last appearance in 1959. 21 years in international squash is probably a record.

The Scottish SRA was formed in October 1936 when its founder members were:

> Aberdeen SRC
> Edinburgh Academicals
> Edinburgh Sports Club
> RAF Turnhouse
> Scottish SRC (Glasgow)
> Watsonians SRC (Edinburgh)

IRELAND

Squash in Ireland has always been closely associated with the Fitzwilliam Lawn Tennis Club in Dublin. In 1902 the Club acquired additional ground in Wilton Place and a pavilion was built there which included what is believed to be the first squash court in Ireland. This had one plaster and three wooden walls. In the twenties a squash tournament was played annually and by 1931 this was recognised as the Irish Championship. The first winner was Arthur Hamilton, who was also a badminton International. The Irish SRA was formed in 1934. It was not until 1937 that the first International match was played by Ireland — against Scotland. Two years later Ireland also met England and Wales, and apart from the War these internationals have been played annually ever since, although there have been two breaks in the Ireland-Wales matches due to the disturbed state of

Ireland.

For a long time there were no purely squash clubs in Ireland, the squash courts being attached to Lawn Tennis clubs such as the Fitzwilliam, or social clubs such as the Kildare Street. But by the middle seventies commercial squash had arrived in Ireland, and the proliferation of courts throughout the Republic as well as in Northern Ireland has had a beneficial effect on the standard of play at all levels.

The Irish Championships have in the main been won by Irishmen, and until the event went Open, the only non-Irish winners were R. Beadle (1952), Gerald Pawle (1938) and W. R. Howson (1952) — all these from England, while in 1949 the Championship was won by A. G. (Bob) Aitchison who represented Scotland. It is perhaps curious that the first winner of the British Amateur Championship, the late T. O. Jameson, never won the Irish title. This may be accounted for by the fact the Irish Championship was not started until nine years after Tommy Jameson had won the Amateur Championship in London. However his son W. S. M. Jameson won the Irish Championship in 1946 and 1947.

Owing to the fact that Eire was neutral in the last War, the Irish Championship was played throughout the thirties and forties without a break. The only other National Championship in Europe where this was done was the Swedish Championship — Sweden being also neutral.

The outstanding player in Ireland over the years has been Donald Pratt who won the Irish Championship ten times between 1957 and 1971 and who played for Ireland on 50 occasions, said to be a world record.

Mention of Irish squash cannot conclude without the name of Barrington cropping up. Jonah went to a prep school in Ireland and after his English public school returned to Ireland as an undergraduate at Trinity College, Dublin, where he had a fairly disastrous year, but played a little mediocre squash. When he was getting good in England in 1965/6 he was offered a place in the Irish team, having a qualification through his father. He had a difficult decison to make — either to play No 1 for Ireland or possibly to get his England 'Cap' at No 5 in the England team. He chose the former and quickly showed his class by taking Jeremy Lyon the England No 1 to five games. He played 10 times for Ireland before turning professional ended his international appearances.

As in Rugby Football, the Irish SRA embraces both Eire and Northern Ireland, and the squash explosion hit Ulster some years before it reached Eire. Indeed, in the late sixties there were as many courts in Ulster as in the whole of Eire. Even the troubled times of the seventies did not dampen the enthusiasm for the game in Ulster and the Ulster Championship, first played in the 1954/5 season has been completed every year since. The most successful competitor has been J. S. Copeland who won it on six occasions between 1957 and 1963.

WALES

Possibly due to the Welsh obsession for rugby football, squash was slow to make an impact in the Principality. In the middle thirties there was one club — the Cardiff SRC — while, rather surprisingly, a country club on the North Wales Coast had two courts. By the time that War broke out, a yacht club, a country club and a golf club, all in South Wales, had each built one court. The Welsh SRA though founded immediately before the War did not get the opportunity of administering the game until after the War and no international matches were played until the 1947/8 season when Scotland and Ireland had easy wins. England did not play Wales until 1951 when putting into court a blockbuster team every member of which was seeded in the Amateur Championship of that year, England won 5-0. The match was played at Cardiff and the Welsh has probably never before seen squash of that level. England have won this annual match every year since with some degree of comfort except for the 1965 match played at Cardiff when Wales won the two top strings, D. B. Hughes beating J. G. A. Lyon and P. D. Stokes beating R. M. H. Boddington. Wales has a fairly even record against Scotland (12 wins, 17 losses), while they have a winning margin of 17 to 10 against Ireland, with two matches unplayed owing to security difficulties. L. J. Verney has been the dominant figure in Welsh squash since the War, his 44 appearances for his country having been spread over 17 years, but the two best players have been Denis Hughes and Peter Stokes, both of whom played also for Great Britain. Hughes lived in the London area and Stokes, an RAF Officer led the usual nomadic existence of service personnel, but as a technician rather than a flying officer, his service was mainly in the UK. He is still playing for his country after 21 years and to date he has played in 52 international matches.

For many years Welsh squash was played almost entirely in the South of the Principality with most of the clubs situated in or near Cardiff, but recently North Wales has shown up strongly. In 1965 there were 27 clubs representing 61 courts in South Wales, with 14 clubs and 30 courts in North Wales. Eleven years later the number of clubs had risen to 53 representing 125 courts. The Cardiff SRC has been the Headquarters of Welsh squash from the beginning but the opening of many new clubs and in particular of the Cardiff Sports Centre with four squash courts has eased the pressure on courts in that city.

The Welsh SRA has always persued an enterprising policy and Welsh teams have constantly visited the continent, sending a team to Scandinavia as far back as 1953. But the rules governing international qualifications resulted in most members of the Welsh team living outside Wales and playing their squash in England. With the recent surge of the game in Wales this is now being rectified.

AUSTRALIA

The absence of British garrisons in Australia delayed the beginnings of the game in that country. Those in India and Egypt had done much to give squash an early start there, but in Australia the start of the game was entirely civilian. In one respect, however, the start was similar to that in India in that the first courts were built by altering a rackets court. This was in the Melbourne Club where the rackets court was built in 1876. The use of the court by rackets players tapered off in 1910 and 1911 so that in 1913 the court was converted into two squash courts of smaller dimensions that those of modern standard courts. But the Melbourne Club was never competitively minded and these courts are not now in use.

The Prince of Wales (later King Edward VIII) was well known to be addicted to squash at which he became a competent performer. On the occasion of his tour to Australia and New Zealand in 1920, a squash court was built in the battlecruiser HMS Renown in which he travelled. This received wide advance publicity and so a gymnasium establishment, Bjelke-Petersen's which had branches in Sydney and Melbourne decided to build a court at their Sydney premises for his use on landing. But the game did not take on here and the court was demolished or burnt down in the mid-twenties. There was also built at the time of the Prince's visit and for his use a private court at the home of Dame Edith Walker at Yaralla.

But the seeds which were sown in Sydney in 1920 did not fall entirely on barren ground and in 1926 the Sydney Squash Club was built with one court, and a court was also built at the Royal Sydney Golf Club in 1929. The rivalry between Sydney and Melbourne finally decided Bjelke-Petersen's to try again, this time at their Melbourne premises, and these courts, owned by Percy Pierce were called Pierce-Bjelke-Petersen's and were built in 1929. From now on, and for many years the emphasis on squash in Australia was centred on Melbourne, and when, in 1934 the Squash Rackets Association of Australia was formed, it was, in fact, a Victoria Association which had been established to serve the interests of local clubs in Melbourne. Ultimately a few interstate clubs were attracted to membership which gave the SRAA a national outlook. Four years later Victoria established its own state body leaving the SRAA to look after the growing national interests.

Before this, however, a narrow court had been built by the Royal Melbourne Tennis Club in 1927, and four years later an extra wide court was built by the Atheneum Club in Melbourne. A court was also built at the Naval and Military Club in the late twenties. In 1931 a court was constructed at Flinders Naval Base at Westernport Bay, Victoria; this was made out of submarine battery cases.

Squash in other states was much slower to get established. In the middle nineteen-thirties courts were built in Perth at the Adelphi and

Esplanade Hotels while in Adelaide the first court was built at the Naval and Military Club.

As long ago as 1925 the Department of Defence showed interest in building courts, but moved somewhat slowly. Having in that year asked the Melbourne Club for the measurements of its court, it was not until six years later that the courts were built at the Victoria Barracks at Sydney. The Air Board were also interested in building courts at various air stations but the only one known to have been built was at the Point Cook air base in Victoria.

The fact that in the early days of squash in Australia, the courts were all found in social or sports clubs undoubtedly hindered the development of the game. In 1955 there were some 50 private and private club courts but only 20 public court establishments. In 1972 there were 1,250 courts distributed among 490 clubs. Most of the courts were public — they could be played on by anyone — and commercially owned. The competitive spirit so dear to the Australian character was catered for by forming clubs within these squash centres. Those wishing to play competition squash joined the club and played in one of the 'pennant' teams — this applies equally to mens and womens teams. I remember visiting a squash centre in North Sydney and being told that they ran a club which had 80 members. On asking how many teams they managed to run I was astounded to be told that the answer was 20! Admittedly in Australia all team events consist of four strings instead of the more usual five. But even so . . . ! In 1972 it was estimated that there were 18,000 players in the country playing in competitions and that the total number of players was 300,000. This means that one person in every 46 of the population played this game. Compare that figure with Great Britain where only one in every 100 plays.

In 1931 the first Amateur Championships were held in Melbourne. While these were really the Victorian Championships, the Victorians christened them the Australian Championships and it was not until 1935 that the two were played independently of each other.

The first Australian Open Championship was played in 1939 and was won by Gordon Watson. This was played annually from 1939 to 1957 excluding the War years 1940-45 as a play off between the Australian Amateur Champion and the Australian Professional Champion. In 1957 it was won by Hashim Khan who was touring Australia at the time. From 1958 to 1969 the event was not played as there were no professionals of any great skill. The Championship was re-commenced in 1970 on a knock-out basis and won by Jonah Barrington. Since that year it has been played at regular intervals and usually won by Geoff Hunt.

In the thirties there was a developing band of professionals attached mainly to the 'gentlemens' clubs which had courts in Melbourne of which the principal were the Athenaeum, the Melbourne and the Naval and Military Clubs.

47

Inter-club competitions were started in Melbourne in the late twenties and early thirties and it was not until 1937 that the first official pennant competition was held consisting mainly of the Sandringham Club, South Yarra Club, Bjelke-Petersen, YMCA, Royal Melbourne Tennis Club and the Naval and Military Club. Pennant competitions commenced in Sydney in 1939.

The standard of play of the leading Australian players before the War suffered from lack of external competition. The first official British team did not visit Australia until 1959 when the standard was just beginning to improve. Two names famous in other games figured prominently in the game in Australia before the War — Don Bradman (cricket) and Harry Hopman (lawn tennis). Sir Donald had the squash misfortunate to live in Adelaide where squash was way behind Melbourne and Sydney. It was said of him that he would have developed greatly had he lived in a squash state like Victoria. Harry Hopman was a better player than Bradman. He was very fit and good at drop shots and lobbing. But neither of these players would be classed as first class by English standards. Brian Burnett, recently President of the SRA recalls that when visiting Australia in the late thirties (as Flight Lieutenant B. K. Burnett he was RAF champion in 1937/38) he played Hopman and although out of practice, beat him easily.

Right from the beginnings of the game in Australia there was 'ball trouble', as in England. Balls were scarce and before the War had to be imported from England. The Silvertown was the popular ball in these pre-War days. It was not until after the War that Slazengers came into the squash ball business in Australia. The only other balls manufactured in Australia in those days were those made by the Ormiston Rubber Company of Victoria, but these balls were of the fast hard American type of ball, popular with what the Australians call "dill-players", but not liked by better players.

There is an interesting letter written by T. H. Prosser and Sons to the Melbourne Club in 1913 apologising for the delay in supplying the club's order of squash balls because of the manufacturers inability to get the suitable rubber for the ball. It was not until after the 1939-45 War that Slazengers came into the squash ball business in Australia. They made the balls and sold them to Dunlops who put their own name on — the very opposite of what took place in England.

In the fifties the late Mervyn Weston and Vin Napier, the latter for many years President of the SRAA as well as one of the leading Australian players did a lot of liaison work with Slazengers to attempt to get away from the "doughy" British ball which they considered ruined stroke play. The result was a harder ball which was eventually accepted worldwide.

The squash boom in the fifties and the enormous increase in the number of squash players in Australia — and to a lesser extent in New Zealand — encouraged the SRAA to invite a British team to tour both these Dominions. There was no doubt that such a tour would be good for squash 'down under' but just how good the Australian top players were compared to the best that Britain could send was a matter of doubt. And Britain certainly sent her best. Nigel Broomfield was the reigning Amateur Champion and three others of the five man team had reached the quarter-finals of the Amateur Championship played some months earlier. The team was captained by Roy Wilson, himself a two time Amateur Champion.

It was soon evident that Australia's best were no match for the visitors. In spite of a very strenuous programme in which 25 matches were played in 41 days every match was won and only one tie was lost. To quote Nigel Broomfield: "During our first few matches against regional sides we met most of the top players in Australia and established a supremacy that was never really disputed".

But the British team were quick to note that some of their younger opponents looked distinctly promising. In particular there was a 21 year old player who scraped into the New South Wales team as No 5 called Hiscoe. Very few would have picked him out as one who would win the British Amateur Championship only three years later.

In the early sixties the power both playing as well as administrative, shifted from Melbourne to Sydney, where the number of courts far outstripped those in Melbourne. These were the days when Ken Hiscoe was amateur champion 1960-67 (except in 1965 when the 18 year old Geoff Hunt captured the title beating Hiscoe in the final). It was in 1965 that the Australian Championships, which always included the Inter-State series, visited Tasmania for the first time.

Australian teams visited England in 1962, 1963 and 1965 and on each occasion easily beat the home team, the start of many years of Australian world wide domination of the game. In 1967 Australia were the hosts for the first International Amateur Championships played under the jurisdiction of the newly formed International Squash Rackets Federation.

The history of the Inter-State matches goes back to 1938 when the first Inter-State match was played at the Royal Sydney Golf Club following the conclusion of the Australian Championships. This was an impromptu match arranged on a friendly basis between New South Wales and Victorian players who had been competing in the championships.

The forerunner of the present series was the match between these same States in 1947 at the University Club, Sydney. In 1951 they were joined by Western Australia in a triangular contest. South Australia joined in in 1953 when the series was played for the first time in Perth. In 1955 these four teams were joined by Queensland and in 1958 by Tasmania. New Zealand was invited to send a team in 1959 (in which year the British touring team also competed), and has sent a team on an invitation basis for many years since then. The Australian Capital Territory was granted 'State' teams status in 1973 and in the following year Northern Territory was admitted.

During all this time New South Wales was able to dominate the series and not even the emergence of Geoff Hunt could loosen the stronghold which that State had on the Trophy. This is hardly surprising considering that the Australian team consisted of three NSW players, plus Hunt. It was only in the early seventies that the magnet of professionalism attracted away from the amateur ranks NSW players such as Hiscoe and Nancarrow, and this led to the emergence of Queensland as the best State.

The rivalry between New South Wales and Victoria, the two chief squash playing States has always been intense. As has been stated, New South Wales outstripped Victoria with Sydney's Vin Napier in command of the SRA of Australia in the mid sixties, followed by another Sydney man, Peter Marsh, the balance of power was tilted in favour of New South Wales. But the big lead in the number of courts by the latter State did not go unchallenged and in 1965 the number of affiliated centres in Victoria, at 79, was only four below the New South Wales figure. Victoria were led by Vic Hunt, father of Geoff and of Geoff's elder brother Bill, who also played in the Victorian team. Vic Hunt, still a fanatically fit man, is nowadays regarded as tɪe greatest living expert on the game in Australia. He was President of the SRA of Victoria for many years. A successful businessman in Melbourne he and SRAV Officers Ian Todd and John Ellery were instrumental in obtaining from the Government a site in Albert Park, on the outskirts of Melbourne on which the SRAV built a squash centre with a large centre court with a gallery capable of holding about 400 spectators and six other courts, and it was here that the Individual Event of the International Championships was played in 1967. Vic Hunt is also an acknowledged expert on the Rules of squash and has served as the Australian representative on the Rules Interpretation Committee of the ISRF since its inception.

Professionalism has never flourished in Australia as it has done in England. Certainly in the thirties there was a developing band of professionals serving the 'gentlemens' clubs in Melbourne in a similar way to those attached to the London West End Clubs. Thus the Royal Melbourne Tennis Club had Jim Watson; the Athenaeum Club had Jock Lyons; the Melbourne Club had John Tunzy and the Naval & Military, Jock Wilson. Gordon Watson also served at some of these clubs. But their numbers were comparatively small.

Jim Watson who won the first Australian Professional Championship in 1931 was noted for his clean hard hitting and was particularly fast. He continued to win this event for eight years before surrendering it to Gordon Watson, who was no relation, and played in this country several times after the War. The entries were small (in 1935 there were only 10) and were mostly from Melbourne. The lack of entries continued after the War and the title was at the mercy of any overseas visiting player who happened to be visiting Australia. Thus in 1949

Mahmoud Kerim won it and in the following year the late Abdul Bari from Bombay. On several occasions the Championship was not held and after 1954 it only took place when overseas players were in the country. It was not held after 1960 when it was won by Hashim's nephew Mohibullah Khan.

CANADA

Squash came to Canada from England in the second half of the nineteenth century and started, as in England, with a number of private courts. More by chance than otherwise the game played was with a soft ball with courts built wider than in the USA. But as there was no controlling body even in England, it is probable that as in that country, the courts and equipment in Canada varied from court to court.

The first recorded courts in Canada were built at the Montreal Racket Club in 1880. They were 19 feet wide and the game was played with the English, or soft ball. The first squash club specially built for the game was the Toronto Racquet Club in 1905. It is on record that here too, the soft ball was used with International scoring, and it appears that it was not until 1919 that the Canadians went over to American balls and scoring. From then until the mid-seventies the games and courts were mainly as in the USA except that the Canadians have never painted the floors white as is done in America.

The Canadian Amateur Singles Championship is one of the earliest national championships to be played, having started in 1912. Players from the US although originally limited to two per year were very often successful and in the long history of this championship it has been won 26 times by a Canadian against 23 times by players from the US. On three occasions, when British teams were touring America, the championship has been won by an English player.

The Canadian Open Championship was not played until 1957 and was starting to attract the Pakistani professionals who visited America every season. It was never won by a Canadian, the Pakistanis scooping the pool every year except in 1959 when it was won by the American Henry Salaun. In 1965 it was amalgamated with the US Open Championship under the title of the North American Open Championship.

Squash was slow to gain popular support and was played mainly in expensive clubs by players who were not overkeen to have the game invaded by players from outside their own social circle. As in the US it was played mainly in the Eastern states although it always had a keen following in British Columbia where for a long time after the rest of Canada had adopted the American game, the International game continued to be played. But even as late as 1971 there were only 42 clubs affiliated to the Canadian SRA of which 26 were in Ontario and nine in British Columbia. Yet by 1976 it was estimated that there were

200 clubs with 350 courts and about 60,000 playing the game. The decision to hold the Amateur International Championships in Canada in 1977 (on International sized courts and under International rules) undoubtedly gave a big fillip to the game there.

From 1947 onwards a number of professional players emigrated to Canada from England and have played a conspicuous part in the development of the game there. In 1976 20 professionals coaching in Canada decided to form their own Association. Before 1976 they were affiliated to the North America Professionals Association.

Of the 85 events featured in the 1976/7 Canadian fixture list 11 were Junior tournaments, 10 doubles events but only seven womens tournaments.

EGYPT

The British presence in Egypt was responsible for the introduction of squash in that country. In Cairo, the Khedivial Sporting Club, later and better known as the Gezira Sporting Club was founded in 1882, while in Alexandria, the Alexandria Sporting Club was founded even earlier, in 1880. Both these clubs built squash courts — originally open air. There is no record of the Egyptians taking to the game at first, but it was useful for squash clubs to have professionals and ball boys, and the first Egyptians to play the game were probably from this category.

One cannot write of Egyptian squash without thinking of the greatest Egyptian squash player Amr Bey later Amr Pasha. Amr was originally a lawn tennis player and first arrived in England as reserve member of the Egyptian Davis Cup team in 1928. It was later as a diplomat and resident in London that he decided to take up squash and it was that great professional 'Oak' Johnson at the RAC who made the young Egyptian into the best player in the world in the thirties. Almost all of his championship successes were gained in England but in 1936 he won the Egyptian Amateur Championship in the first year it was played. It was the only time he competed in the event and (except during the War when the Championship was not held) British serving officers almost monopolised the Championship until 1949, since when Egyptians have provided the winners every year.

For some years after the War the best player was Mohmoud Kerim who won the British Open Championship on four occasions. Curiously he did not play in the Egyptian Professional Championship and his name does not appear as the winner of any Egyptian national championship.

It was only after the War that the Egyptians took up squash seriously and it was in January 1951 that a team of four representing the Heliopolis Sporting Club arrived in England. Although it contained Mohsen Nour, an ex-Egyptian Amateur Champion, the exceptionally cold weather they met, and the small time allowed for acclimatisation proved too much. They played in the Amateur championship with limited success and also competed in the South of England Championship.

By the early fifties, numerous courts and clubs were being constructed with the Army leading the way. The Army Sports Federation had 10 courts on the outskirts of Cairo while the Directorate of Physical Training built six courts at the Ministry of Education. Gezira by this time had eight courts and their great rivals the Heliopolis Sporting Club had four. In Alexandria the Sporting Club had six courts.

It was perhaps hardly surprising that all this squash activity produced some good players and in January 1956 Ibrahim Amin, unseeded, won the British Amateur Championship. No Egyptians came over in 1957 — the year of Suez — but six entered in the following year and Egyptians have competed in force ever since, winning the Amateur Championship twice and providing the runner-up on seven occasions. Egyptians were also successful in the Open Championship, Mahmoud Kerim winning four times and Abou Taleb three times.

By the middle sixties, Egypt boasted three courts capable of holding nearly 500 spectators — two in Cairo and the other in Alexandria. Plans to build a mammoth court at the Gezira Club were designed by T. Shafik, an army architect who was three times runner-up in the British Amateur Championship but a period of economic stringency held the project up and it has never been built.

Since 1973 large numbers of young Egyptians have been coming to England each year for the Amateur Championship — 18 in 1976 — and the standard of their play is steadily improving.

EUROPE

Europe has been strangely backward in promoting squash. While before the War there were courts attached to clubs which dealt mainly with other games such as lawn tennis and real tennis (Paris), there were few if any clubs devoted entirely to squash.

Yet there were signs in the late twenties and the thirties that squash was experiencing on a small scale the boom which was at that time taking place in England. It is not easy to pinpoint the earliest court in Europe, but the Societe de Jeu de Paume et de Racquets in Paris turned its rackets court into four squash courts in the late twenties and must be one of, if not the earliest squash club in Europe. Most squash courts on the Continent built before the War have survived and are in use today.

In Germany there were courts at Dusseldorf before the War and which have disappeared — possibly bombed. In Berlin there was in the middle thirties a squash club — the Erster Squash Club von

Deutschland which had only one court. This has disappeared but another club, founded in 1939, as mentioned later in this chapter, was more fortunate.

Squash in Europe has been at best sporadic. In Northern Europe which has a climate ideal for the game, its spread was for many years disappointing. Up to 1939 there was a club in each of the following countries — Belgium, Denmark, France, Germany, Holland, Portugal, Sweden and Switzerland. Of these countries Denmark and Holland were more advanced than the others.

The most disappointing country is Denmark where there were more courts before the War than there are today. The first club built in the mid-thirties was situated on the West side of Copenhagen and consisted of three courts. These were built by international tennis player Helge Ploughman and his brother but did not attract sufficient support and were dismantled. In the meantime the enthusiasm of the Ploughmans had succeeded in getting a further three courts built in Vestersohus, a large block of flats in the centre of Copenhagen and these have survived to this day and are the headquarters of squash in Denmark. Several other clubs were built in and around Copenhagen but the game never 'took off' and most of the courts were either dismantled or used for table tennis. The three clubs in Denmark in the forties and immediately after the War — the Kobenhauns Squash Klub, Kobenhauns, Boldklub's Squash Club and ·the Arbejdernes Tennis Club failed to get squash recognised by the main Danish sporting authority (Dansk Idratsforbund) and it has been the lack of foresight by this body that has prevented the development of squash in Denmark.

The KSK however continued manfully and after the War established contact with the SRA in England as a result of which an invitation was accepted to send an England side to Copenhagen in March 1949. The strength of the Danes was in some doubt although one of them, B. O. Smitt had played without success in the Amateur Championship three months earlier. England won easily, the Danes being unlucky in losing their top string by illness immediately prior to the match. The SRA invited Denmark to visit England in the next season and in November they arrived and after matches against Scotland, the North of England and the Midlands, tried conclusions against England in London. In spite of having won so easily in Copenhagen, England put into court the strongest team available and gave the Danes a terrible drubbing. It was obvious that Denmark was not up to international standard and the fixture has not been renewed. England did not meet Denmark again until the European Championships in 1973.

Although Denmark did not play England for over 20 years, annual matches were played against Sweden starting from 1939. The best player produced by Denmark has been Peter Gerlow who as a boy won the Drysdale Cup in England in 1961 and 1962. He would have been a very good player indeed had he had the opportunity of regular play in England. Nils Middelboe deserves mention as the most enthusiastic player in Denmark who represented his country many times, even after he had attained veteran status.

SRA and club teams have visited Denmark on a number of occasions and the results of European Championship matches have shown that at last enthusiasm and the resulting standard of play is on the up grade again. One cannot conclude any account of Danish squash without mention of the doubles game which has thrived in that country, although in singles courts. The Doubles Championship is an important and enjoyable part of the National Championships at which the Danes have always excelled.

Belgium is another country which has been lagging behind in the squash boom. For many years there was a club in Brussels with four courts opened in 1939 in the Shell building. Belgium has never played international matches against England but has played matches annually against Holland. For some years after the War, Belgian players used to compete in the British Amateur Championship, but after that generation had grown too old there was no follow through. Only starting in the second year of the European Championships did Belgium enter a team, the majority of whom were Englishmen living in Belgium. There have recently been signs, however, of a resurgence of squash activity in Belgium.

Immediately after the War two courts were constructed on the premises of the Beerschot Club in Antwerp but by 1970 these had fallen into disuse and in the same year the Brussels Squash Rackets Club were told by Shell that their lease would not be renewed. The Club was fortunate in being able to build five courts in the grounds of the Royal Leopold Tennis Club on the outskirts of Brussels. The Club was destroyed by fire in 1976. Two other clubs built a total of five squash courts, which were opened in 1974, and with the formation of a national squash rackets federation squash began to participate in the squash boom which was sweeping Europe.

The lack of activity in Belgium is all the more surprising in that next door in Holland there is a boom in the game. In 1934 there was a one court club at Utrecht and later clubs were opened in Rotterdam (three courts) and Amsterdam (one court), but since the War the headquarters of the game have been at the Hague SRC whose two courts (increased to four in 1973) have been the venue of the Dutch International Championship since its inception in 1963. The SRA annually send four top players to this event which has always been won by a British International player. Many other players from England make what has become an annual pilgrimage to this pleasant club in rural surroundings on the outskirts of the Hague, attracted by the hospitality of the Dutch hosts and the excellence of the squash. In 1973, out of a draw of 64, 40 were from England.

A series of promising Dutch junior players has been sent over to

England to compete in the Drysdale Cup and while none have succeeded in winning it, Holland has more than once provided the runner-up. Some of these players have gone on to win the Dutch Amateur Championship one of which R. J. Anjema has been Amateur Champion for eight years, although he has a long way to go to equal the record of A. G. Maris who won this championship for 15 years in succession from 1946 to 1960. Prior to the European Championships, England played Holland only once, in 1953, winning easily. Aided by excellent publicity the game is expanding rapidly and by the end of 1978 there were over 100 courts in operation.

West Germany is a country in which one would imagine squash would flourish but only recently has any real progress been made. Before the War there was a one court club in Berlin and in 1939 a club with four courts was opened in the grounds of Siemens the electrical company, for the benefit of the Company's staff. It appears that Herr Siemen junior was up at Oxford in the mid-thirties and took to the game there, so that on his return to Germany he persuaded his father to build a squash club. Although in the centre of Berlin and surrounded by devastation caused by allied bombing, the club, the Squash Club Siemens-Worke, miraculously escaped. In 1947 when I captained the first Escorts club team to visit the BAOR we played a match there. It was fortunate that the club was situated just inside the British Zone and the courts were used continuously by the British forces of occupation in Berlin. But there were difficulties. At one period the lights, which were controlled from the Russian sector, were only permitted between the hours of 1.00 a.m. and 4.00 a.m. which imposed a considerable strain on the enthusiasm of even the most ardent players. The club is now flourishing.

Attempts to get the game started in the past have been frustrated by bureaucratic hinderance but in 1969 a four court club was opened in Hamburg and by 1973 the prospects were sufficiently good to warrant the formation of a national association. By 1976 there were over 20 courts open in Hamburg alone and clubs have also been opened in Munich, Dusseldorf and Cologne. German Television has been helpful in introducing the game and has covered the opening of squash centres in Hamburg, and other cities. By mid 1978 over 70 centres were open, comprising 400 courts, nearly all built in less than two years — the most spectacular advance in the history of the game.

West Germany hosted the European championships in 1979 and have applied for membership of the ISRF.

BAOR — The tedium of garrison duty was relieved for many by the squash facilities provided by the Army and the RAF. The courts were in many cases rather makeshift, many being constructed inside large German barns in which the gallery was 40 feet above the level of the court, and approached by a ladder, but proper courts were built at the BAOR Headquarters first at Bad Oeynhausen and later at Munchen Gladbach. By 1949 over 40 courts had been constructed in various parts of Germany. Touring teams such as the Escorts and the Jesters were made welcome. In 1949 a quadrangular tournament took place at Minden (the teams in order of success were: RAF, Escorts, Brussels and Combined Services (Germany)). This led eventually to the BAOR Easter Festival played annually over the Easter week-end. Visiting teams vary from year to year but the Escorts and the Jesters generally send teams, and others have been Wales, Holland and Denmark.

Sweden, now the leading squash nation on the Continent of Europe started slowly. A rather sumptuous three court club was built in Stockholm in the early thirties with the walls made of powdered marble. During the War neutral Sweden was almost cut off and while squash continued to be played throughout the War — Sweden and Ireland were the only countries in the world whose national championships continued to be played during the War years — the main trouble in Sweden was the shortage of balls. RAF planes occasionally landed in Stockholm with diplomats and despatches and there was an arrangement under which the pilots used to bring with them boxes of squash balls which just kept the game alive. For years after the War there was little expansion. A single court at a hotel in Linkoping about 100 miles south of Stockholm was the only addition to the Swedish squash facilities until the arrival of Jan Landvik. Learning his squash at the Stockholm SC he realised the enormous possibilities of the game, and he decided to build a squash complex and promote the game using modern marketing techniques. And so was born in 1968 the Kungstenshallen Squash Banor, with five courts where anyone can play from 7.00 a.m. to 11.00 p.m. The Wasa Squash Club has its own clubroom next to the courts for its members who use the public courts and have certain booking rights. An Egyptian ex-amateur international was installed as professional. The success of this enterprise was immediate and encouraging. And so Jan planned and built courts all over Sweden. By 1976 there were 400 courts in 66 squash centres.

Slowly the standard of play rose. The Swedish SRA paid particular attention to the coaching of young players and sent teams of juniors to England to play in the Drysdale Cup and other junior competitions. In the 1976 European Championships Sweden came third, above Ireland and Wales and in the following year came second to England. In the International Amateur Championships in England in the same year Sweden came sixth out of 10, but in the Individual event Swedish players won the final of both Plate events. Swedish players also performed well in the British Amateur Championship in that year.

Squash Courts in Southern Europe have been few and far between but mention must be made of Monaco. The Monte Carlo Country Club built squash courts in the twenties when squash was played mainly in the season from January to April. After the War the courts were hardly used but Prince Rainier who had his private court in the Palace grounds and Aris Vatembella who had played squash all round the Mediterranean revived the game and started the Monte Carlo

SRC.

Finland is geographically out on a limb but proximity to Sweden has been a help and starting in 1967 the game made remarkably rapid strides. Squash facilities are on the Swedish lines being open to all but with a club at each centre.

Realising the need for competition Finnish players started playing in the British Amateur Championship in 1971 and have competed regularly in the European Championships with some success, coming fourth in 1978.

Harri Salo has been Finland's most consistent native born player but has now been overtaken by several younger players.

Switzerland — For many years squash in Switzerland consisted of the one court owned by the La Cotiere Squash Club and built originally for the staff of the United Nations Secretariat. In 1972 the Geneva SRC opened with three courts and with further clubs opening in Geneva and Zurich the game expanded rapidly. Swiss television has done much to popularise the game and in 1974 a Swiss Open Championship was launched which attracted a strong overseas entry. Commercial and civic sponsorship helped to make the event a success.

France has been a disappointing country squashwise. The Societe Sportive de Jeu de Paume et de Racquets has four cement floored courts in the centre of Paris, the membership of which was mainly composed of British and American residents of Paris. Then, in 1974 British property developers, Town & Country who had built a number of courts in England startled the squash world by digging out a squash club with six courts under a skyscraper in Paris. The club was said to have cost £800,000 and it is difficult to see how it could ever have paid its way. Unfortunately the property company collapsed and the club was advertised for sale at £1,000,000. It is still on the market but the club is flourishing while a number of clubs have recently been opened in various parts of France, so that by the end of 1978 there were over 70 courts in operation.

The European Federation — The rather stringent, even if necessary, qualifications for membership of the International Squash Rackets Federation led the SRA to hold a meeting of representatives of the various nations taking part in the first European Championships with a view to forming a European Federation. There were 11 countries competing in the Championships, held in Edinburgh in April 1973, and two countries not competing, Spain and Switzerland sent observers. At this meeting the decision was taken to form the European Squash Rackets Federation. From the outset it was made clear that there would be close co-operation with the ISRF, whose secretary also attended the meeting. A number of European national associations would be members of both Federations, but unlike the ISRF membership of the ESRF would not be restricted to countries which had a national association. The four constituent countries of Great Britain have individual membership of the ESRF. The main function of the Federation is to act as the focal point for the stimulation and development of the game on the Continent. The ISRF welcomed the new Federation and its representative has attended meetings of the ISRF.

There were seven founder members — England, Finland, Ireland, Netherlands, Scotland, Sweden and Wales. Within a few years the following countries had been added: Belgium, Denmark, France, Western Germany, Gibraltar, Greece, Luxembourg, Malta, Monaco, Spain and Switzerland.

Meetings of the Federation have been held annually since 1973 concurrently with the European Championships which have been held as follows:

1973	Edinburgh	1977	England
1974	Sweden	1978	Holland
1975	Ireland (Dublin)	1979	Germany
1976	Belgium		

It has been one of the duties of the Federation to fix the venues of future European Championships, which in 1973 were sponsored by Target Trust and for the next three years by Pilkington Glass. In 1978 the main sponsor was Dunlops.

European Championships — The first European Championships were held in Edinburgh in April 1973. Ten teams entered, divided into two pools. The four home countries supplied the winners and runners-up of both pools. In the final between the pool winners England easily beat Scotland 5-0 and in the match between the runners-up, Ireland beat Wales 4-1. In 1974 the Championships were held in Sweden. The number of teams competing increased to twelve. The results were the same as in the previous year except that in the match between the pools runners-up Ireland beat Wales 5-0.

The third European Championships were held in Dublin in April 1975. The event was again divided into two pools but at the conclusion of the pools each team played its opposite number in the other pool, thus producing a finishing order for all the teams. The Swedes showed the results of their dedication and perseverence by beating both Ireland and Wales and the final order was: 1. England; 2. Scotland; 3. Sweden; 4. Ireland; 5. Wales; 6. Finland; 7. Denmark; 8. Belgium; 9. Netherlands; 10. Switzerland; 11. Germany; 12. France.

The 1976 championships were held in Brussels and an increase in the number of teams to 15 increased the number of pools to four. Sweden confirmed their advance and again came third behind England and Scotland. The final positions were: 1. England; 2. Scotland; 3. Sweden; 4. Ireland; 5. Wales; 6. Denmark; 7. Finland; 8. Netherlands; 9. Belgium; 10. Switzerland; 11. France; 12. Germany; 13. Greece; 14. Luxemburg; 15. Monaco.

England played host to the 1977 championships which were held in Sheffield. Sweden again advanced, coming second to England. The final positions were: 1. England; 2. Sweden; 3. Scotland; 4. Ireland; 5. Finland; 6. Wales; 7. Netherlands; 8. Belgium; 9. Switzerland; 10. Denmark; 11. France; 12. Germany; 13. Greece.

In 1978 the European Championships moved to the Netherlands and while the Dutch authorities worked wonders at the Amstelveen Club, near Amsterdam, they were badly let down by the ESRF who had undertaken the task of finding sponsors for the event and finally could provide sponsorship covering only 20% of the cost of running the Championships, leaving the Dutch SRA with a loss of £7,000.

Italy and Luxemburg entered teams so that there were again 15 teams. An innovation was the inclusion of a Ladies Championship in which 11 teams competed. England won easily.

The final positions in the Mens event were: 1. England; 2. Sweden; 3. Scotland; 4. Finland; 5. Ireland; 6. Netherlands; 7. Wales; 8. Belgium; 9. Germany; 10. Denmark; 11. Switzerland; 12. France; 13. Greece; 14. Italy; 15. Luxemburg.

INDIA

Squash was introduced to India by the British who built squash courts all over the country to keep its Service personnel in top condition. Since then the game has progressed considerably and today squash courts are to be found in the most remote parts of India. With distances being vast, it is not easy to determine the present number of squash courts, but at a reasonable estimate, the number of courts under the control of the Services Sports Control Board could be well over 500.

The British officers who were members of the social-cum-sports Clubs introduced squash to these Clubs. Every high class club in India now has squash courts which are well patronised.

Squash found its way into Indian schools which were modelled on English Public Schools. Squash Courts are found in Dehra Dunn Public School, Mayo College Ajmer, the Daly College Indore, Shivaji Military College Poona, Bai Lakshmibai College of Physical Education Gwalior, etc.

Later on, squash courts were built on the various University campuses. Every year Inter-University Championships are held at different Universities by rotation and at least ten Universities participate in the championships.

The Squash Rackets Association of India was founded in 1953 and six major squash championships are held annually under its jurisdiction. The Western India championships are held in Bombay, the East India Championships in Calcutta, the Central India Championships at the Daly College, Indore and the Maharashtra State at Deolali. The Delhi State Squash Rackets Championships are held in Delhi. The National championships are played in Bombay, Calcutta, and Delhi every year by rotation.

The Services Sports Control Board organises various command championships and just prior to the National Championships it holds Services Championships.

Because of the vast distances involved, few players except those living close to the championships compete in the regional tournaments. Promising young players suffer greatly from a lack of top class competitive experience and even more from the lack of coaching. Squash in India has been dominated by the Army which for many years produced the winners of the national championships. In recent years the most successful player has been Anil Nayar who, as a boy, came to England and won the Drysdale Cup in 1965. Later he spent some years in the USA and was the leading amateur in that country becoming National Champion in 1969 and 1970 before returning to India where he has won the All-India Championships on six occasions.

Indian teams have competed with moderate success on some occasions in the International Amateur Championships but their participation has been limited by currency difficulties and the hard line attitude of their Government on the South African problem.

KENYA

As in many other parts of the British Colonial Empire, squash came early to Kenya and the first courts were constructed at the Muthaiga Club on its formation on the outskirts of Nairobi as long ago as 1912, with the first tournament being played here in 1914 for a trophy presented by Captain Schwartze. After 1937 this tournament was held only spasmodically but in 1972, to mark the 60th anniversary of the Club, the tournament was reinstated and in that year was won by British player John Easter who was on a coaching tour. Meantime the cup became recognised as the All Kenya Squash Rackets Challenge Cup.

But in the early days of squash in Kenya squash courts were constructed up and down the country well before the 1914-18 Great War. Many of them were rough open courts erected by the District Commissioners in small government stations where the number of resident whites was probably less than a dozen. Many were at an altitude of up to 9,000 feet at which height the ball bounces prodigiously. Perhaps the loneliest court was that at Mandera on the Ethiopean and Somali border, 650 miles away from civilization, when the shade temperature regularly goes up to over 100°F. Other courts at the coast posed different problems for here while the temperature averaged about 80°F the main drawback was the high humidity. The fact that there were a number of courts prior to 1914 is remarkable considering that it was only in 1899 that the railway from the coast reached the "bleak, swampy stretch of soppy landscape, windswept, devoid of human habitation — the resort of thousands of wild

61

animals''. This is a description of the gound on which the city of Nairobi now stands. The white inhabitants of Kenya at that time had come mainly from upper class England and so were more likely to have played squash in England.

As Kenya grew, so did squash. In 1961 there were 21 affiliated clubs containing 23 courts. Growth in the fifties had been restricted by the Mau Mau Emergency. Later the granting of independence and the consequent reduction in the European population further restricted the growth of the game, but by 1974 there were approximately 60 courts in the country of which half were in the Nairobi district.

Most of the larger towns boast a court, frequently as a relic of colonial times. Local hazards on some of these courts include the sun, rain, hyraxes, snakes, geckos and termites. But these do not stop the players, except perhaps temporarily!

In the 1939-45 War there were many instances of play being interrupted by enemy action, but at Mandera, mentioned above, it was not unusual for the players to be warned that a border raid was imminent. One officer who was playing at the time was reported to have told the police sergeant who had warned him: "I'll finish my game first". Shades of Drake!

By 1952 squash had spread up and down the country sufficiently to warrant the formation of a national association. Dr F. M. D. Flowerdew, twice a semi-finalist in the British Amateur Championships before the War, and five times champion of Kenya, took a leading part in the formation of the Kenya Squash Rackets Association which was modelled on the SRA and affiliated to it. Kenya has the geographical advantage of being on the route from England to South Africa and the KSRA has on several occasions entertained national teams on their way to and from South Africa. There are not yet any resident professionals in the country and the KSRA has always persued a forward policy in obtaining the services of British leading players for a few weeks coaching. After he had turned professional, Jonah Barrington 'discovered' Kenya as providing ideal training ground for his championships. If he could successfully put through a rigorous training schedule on the slopes of Mount Kenya at a height of some 7,000 feet he found he would be super fit at sea level. In return he willingly gave clinics and exhibition matches which improved the standard of play in the country.

NEW ZEALAND

Squash came comparatively late to New Zealand. The records of early organised squash were destroyed in the War, but it seems that the earliest court was built in the Christchurch (South Island) Club and it was here that the first national championship was played in 1932. It is not recorded how many entries there were but the championship was won by G. E. F. Kingscote who was recognised as the 'father' of squash in New Zealand. Mr Kingscote had learned his squash at the Bath Club in England and introduced to New Zealand two important and hitherto unknown shots to the game there — the drop shot and the kill into the nick. We are not informed what ball was played with at this time and from the fact that the drop shot was unknown it is possible that the hard 'nigger' ball was used.

Meantime in the North Island, the Royal Navy had built two courts at the Devonport Naval Base at Auckland. The first New Zealand Association was formed in 1932 with Officers from both North and South Islands.

1933 was an important year in New Zealand squash with the opening of the first Public (or open) Club at Timaru, while in the following year the game had made sufficient strides to warrant sending some players to compete in the Australian Championships held that year at Melbourne. They did pretty well with P. D. Hall, the first secretary of the NZSRA reaching the final and D. W. J. Gould (Christchurch) the semi-final. Both these players were defeated by Harry Hopman, of Davis Cup fame.

During the pre-War days the Association acted solely to organise New Zealand tournaments. The National Championship continued to be played at Christchurch for four years and its venue was then moved to Timaru also in South Island where it was played until 1939 when it moved to the Devonport Naval Base, the first time it was played in North Island. Since its inception the venue has been chosen fairly evenly between the two islands.

The second New Zealand SRA was formally incorporated in 1939 (the first one had been unincorporated) with the object of controlling, advancing and regulating the game throughout the country — objects far wider than those of the original Association. During the War it was of necessity dormant, but a meeting was held in June 1946 with fifteen members divided into three classes — Open Clubs (4), Armed Services courts (5) and private court owners (6).

In 1948 it was decided to establish the office of the Association each year at the club holding the Championships for the year. Hardly surprisingly this system was not found entirely satisfactory and in 1953 it was decided to establish the registered office in Palmerston North, with Roy Haddon as Secretary. If ever a man deserved the title 'Mr Squash', that man was Roy Haddon. He was fanatically keen on the game. A chartered accountant by profession, the wonder was that he was ever able to devote sufficient time to run his firm, so much of his time was taken up with squash administration. When he became honorary secretary the NZSRA had 800 members. When he died in 1975, appropriately playing in a squash tournament, aged 67, the membership had risen to 23,000. His best memorial was the ISRF Championships held in New Zealand in 1971 which he entirely organised. He came to England in 1969 as manager of the New

Zealand team for the Amateur International Championships of that year. If his devotion to the game occasionally overran his discretion, any annoyance caused thereby was of short duration.

It was in 1953, when Roy Haddon became secretary, that the NZSRA was put on a firm financial footing by the introduction of an annual levy on all players, the funds thereby raised to be used for any purpose promoting squash including loans to new clubs and subsidising expenses to teams travelling overseas.

New Zealand became a Founder Member of the ISRF on its formation in 1967. In its early days, the NZSRA adopted an independent attitude as far as the Rules of the Game were concerned and did not follow all the rules laid by by the SRA! For instance, there was no appeal by a player for a let, the granting of such being entirely at the discretion of the marker, nor was the new rule passed in 1948 (by which a point could be awarded against an obstructing player) followed in New Zealand.

New Zealand's geographical isolation meant that it was some time before overseas teams visited the dominion and it was not until 1953 that a New Zealand representative team toured Australia, and 1958 before an Australian team visited New Zealand. The British team which toured Australia in 1959 made a short tour of New Zealand on their way home.

The International Amateur Championships were held in New Zealand in 1971 and this undoubtedly gave a great fillip to the game there. New Zealand has sent a team to all these championships, and there can be no doubt that this participation has improved the standard of play of their top players.

In 1975 New Zealand took over the administration of the International Squash Rackets Federation under the chairmanship of Mr Murray C. Day of Hamilton.

In 1976 the number of affiliated clubs had risen to 140 and the number of registered players to 38,366.

M. Dardir the Egyptian professional for some years resident in Australia toured New Zealand in 1963 and in several subsequent years, finally settling there in 1967 as Resident Coach.

Womens squash in New Zealand, although it lagged behind the mens game, is now firmly established. The Womens Championship was started in 1951 and has been played regularly since then. In the early days the most successful competitor was Mrs N. New who was successful on four occasions, while in more recent times Mrs P. Buckingham has been the most successful player and has also won the Championship four times.

PAKISTAN

Squash was introduced to Pakistan by Officers of the Indian Army and squash courts were built at the recreational and social clubs built in the garrison towns of the North West Frontier Province. Some of these clubs originally built rackets courts, but the expense of this game prevented all but a few from playing it, and with the increasing popularity of squash a number of the rackets courts were converted into squash courts. It was the markers at these clubs who turned from rackets to squash and who were the founders of the dynasty of squash professionals, which were later to achieve world wide fame. Most (but not all) of the Pakistani professionals are descendants of Rehmatullah who was the Imam or prayer leader of Peshawar, or of Muhammad Ali, and these two families were connected by marriage.

But the game was still exclusive. After the British withdrawal from India and the founding of Pakistan, membership of the social clubs at Karachi and other centres became increasingly Pakistani, but it was not until 1953 that the first Pakistan Amateur Championship was played. The leading amateur was A. J. Quraishi who also acted as Secretary of the Pakistan SRA, and who now teaches in Nigeria.

In those early days the main centre was the second city in Pakistan, Lahore, where the game was played on the two rather broken down courts of the old Punjab Club. By 1957 there were still only 15 regular players there. In the following year the Lahore SRA was formed and when the Pakistan Administrative Staff College took over the Punjab Club the squash courts were leased to the LSRA. Gradually the number of courts increased — some new ones were built, but many were old courts which were renovated and brought into use. During the decade 1954-64, 20 courts were constructed in West Pakistan. The Colleges authorities were not slow to recognise the merits of the game and in 1961 all the colleges told their students that they could play without any payment, with balls and rackets supplied also free.

A milestone in Pakistan squash was the visit of a British team in November 1963. In August of that year the Pakistan SRA invited the SRA to send a team to compete in the Pakistan Amateur Championships but owing to the short time available and the absence of any travel expenses, the invitation was declined. This disappointed the Pakistanis who voiced their displeasure, a short account of which found its way into "The Times". Their argument was that every year the best Pakistanis visited England for the purpose of playing in the chief British tournaments so why couldn't the British reciprocate. The dispatch in The Times caught the eye of the Chairman of Godfrey Phillips, the tobacco firm, who contacted the SRA and offered to defray the expenses of a four-man team — as far as is known this was the earliest example of commercial sponsorship of squash. The British team consisted of D. B. Hughes, the British and Welsh International, J. F. Skinner, T. D. Gathercole and P. H. Fuente. There can be no doubt that the British presence added to the interest of the Pakistan Championships. There were 44 entries for the Amateur Championship, 20 for the Junior Championship and 16 for the Professional Championship. The British players had not had time to get thoroughly acclimatised, but Hughes reached the quarter-finals before being beaten by Khalid Mir 9-1, 6-9, 9-5, 6-9, 9-6. The Pakistani went on to defeat Skinner in the semi-finals by 9-6, 9-6, 8-10, 9-5. The final was won by Aftab Jawaid who beat Khalid Mir 9-5, 9-2, 9-0, and went on to win the British Amateur Championship a few weeks later.

But in spite of the successes of Hashim and his fellow Khans, and the efforts of the educational authorities to popularise the game, amateur squash did not catch on in Pakistan until the Pakistan Air Force took over the administration of the game. Air Marshal Nur Khan retired from the PAF and became Chairman of Pakistan International Airlines and established squash camps for the leading amateur players whom he enrolled on the PIA payroll. Players like Qamar Zaman, Mohibullah Khan and Gogi Alauddin derived immense benefits from this convenient arrangement and between them carved up most of the leading amateur championships all over the world. For a time the success of some of the leading players from Lahore was halted by a dispute between the Lahore SRA and the Pakistan SRF, as a result of which the former was disaffiliated, but peace was happily restored after two or three years and Gogi Alauddin, Hiddy Jahan and Sajjad Muneer were received back into the fold.

There was however a constant drain on Pakistan's leading players as the benefits of professionalism lured some away, but the far sighted policy of PIA in encouraging promising youngsters resulted in a steady stream of top class juniors coming on to make good any gaps caused by the departure of leading amateurs into the professional ranks.

By 1976 the number of courts in the country had risen to 120. As the PSRF report to the ISRF stated: "The game was not that much popular . . . this being a costly game, it was not played by common men and was restricted to the cantonment area".

SOUTH AFRICA

Squash started slowly in South Africa where the first courts were constructed in about 1906 at the Johannesburg Country Club and at the Pretoria Club. These were open courts, longer and wider than the present day standard sizes. They were really bat fives courts. It was not until 1930 that the Johannesburg Country Club court was roofed and reduced to the present standard size. It is interesting to note that the plaster put on to this court in 1930 is still in excellent condition. From 1925 the game increased in popularity with many courts being built in clubs in Johannesburg, Cape Town and Durban.

Apart from the USA where the first amateur championship was played in 1906, South Africa claims the earliest championship, started in 1910 at the Johannesburg Country Club. The donor of the cup, T. C. Wolley Dodd stipulated that the championship should always be played at the club of the holder, and for this reason the Championships were held at the Country Club until 1926 when it was won by Michael McMaster who later became Chairman of Slazengers Ltd. He came from Durban and the Championship was played there for four years before, with the first win of H. W. P. Whiteley the venue returned to Johannesburg where it remained until 1951 when the Championship was held at the Kelvin Grove Club, Cape Town. The SRA of Southern Africa which had been formed in 1948 then decided that the Championships should be moved around from place to place, and in 1953 they were held at the Salisbury Sports Club as part of the Rhodesia Centenery celebrations. When the SRA of Southern Africa was formed its jurisdiction extended to Rhodesia in addition to Botswana and Swaziland.

The chief club in South Africa for many years was the famous Wanderers Club in Johannesburg where a large number of different sports are catered for. Prior to 1952 this club only had two squash courts but in that year a new block of five courts was built which created the best venue for Championship squash and the South Africa Championships were played chiefly here until 1972. The main court had a gallery which could accommodate 400 spectators, making it for many years the largest gallery in the world. The South African Championships are now played at the Witwatersrand University, the courts at which have been modernised and have even better gallery accommodation.

South African squash owes a great debt to Bill Whiteley, an Englishman who learnt his squash at Clifton College before emigrating to South Africa in 1930. In addition to winning the South African Championships eight times, he became the first Chairman of the SRA of SA and continued as such for twelve years. In 1956-57 he captained the South African team which visited England in that season. He did not play in the Test Matches but played in nine of the other matches. He was already a veteran and nothing gave him greater pleasure during the tour than winning the Amateur Veterans Championship, which he accomplished without losing a game.

The best players in the fifties were the Callaghan brothers; Brian won the Championship on five occasions, Denis on only two. Brian however never came to England whereas Denis played first string for the South African touring team in England in 1956-7. He never succeeded in beating Roy Wilson but in the final of the Amateur Championship Denis won the first two games, and it was only a fine exhibition of guts which saw Wilson win 9-6 in the fifth game. Eleven years later these two played each other in the final of the Amateur Veterans Championship in London, Wilson again winning after losing the first game to love.

With the proliferation of overseas tours, the South African title frequently went to visiting players and among these have been Broomfield, Oddy, Barrington and Ayton from England and Hiscoe and Nancarrow from Australia.

In 1955 the SRA accepted the invitation of the SRA of Southern Africa to send a team to that country to play a series of four Test Matches as well as eleven other matches. The British team captained by Norman Borrett was criticised as containing too many old players and certainly Borrett, B. C. Phillips and A. T. Seymour Hayden were past their best. Perhaps the strength of the opposition to be met was underestimated. Certainly the drubbing given to the team by the South Africans was severe — South Africa won three out of the four Tests. It was significant that the only British win was at sea level at Durban.

The following year South Africa was invited to a return contest in England. The British team was much younger than that which had been defeated in the previous year and after a narrow victory in the first Test went on to win the next two convincingly. For some years Great Britain continued its run of success but in 1970 South Africa had a decisive 3-0 win in a Test series played in South Africa.

For many years progress of squash in South Africa was hindered by the fact that it was played only in clubs, but in 1975 the first 'public courts' complex was opened at Randburg, a suburb of Johannesburg, and other similar centres were built thereafter by the same syndicate at Cape Town and Johannesburg.

A branch of the Jesters Club was started in South Africa in 1957, the membership of which is currently over 170. A few years later a branch of the Escorts was also formed in Johannesburg and its members, who now number well over 100, have spread all over the Republic.

Squash in South Africa as well as South African teams proceeding overseas have been bedevilled by the policies of the South African Government in connection with apartheid, and even more so by the attitude of other countries towards South African participation in sport.

The SRA of Southern Africa issued a statement in April 1976 pointing out that in their Constitution there is no restriction as to the race or colour of those eligible for membership. The Association states however that up to that time the South African natives in South Africa have exhibited virtually no interest in the game. There are a few Indian teams playing league squash, particularly in Durban, but courses, clinics and lectures organised by the Association aimed specifically at interesting coloureds in the game have met with little success. Once interest is shown the Association states that there is nothing to stop coloureds playing with persons of all races and, if invited, being selected as members of the national team.

CHAPTER V

THE NORTH AMERICAN
GAME

*A*S IN England, the early days of squash in America are 'lost in the mists of antiquity'. Yet it seems tolerably certain that the first squash court was built at the Racquet Club, Walnut Street, Philadelphia shortly after 1890. The Clubhouse had been opened that year with two racquets courts and the squash court was built shortly after. It was squeezed in under the roof and at the back of one of the racquets courts. One could only get into the court by walking along beams of the roof and there was no gallery. The size of the court was probably dictated by the amount of space available and was somewhat smaller, at 31 feet by 17 feet 6 inches, than the modern American court. But is was 10 years later before a club championship was held.

About the same time that the Philadelphia court was built, there was erected in the 43rd Street clubhouse of the New York Racquet and Tennis Club a court which at first was called a fives court. This court however was never used for fives but was probably used for squash tennis, a game which was played a good deal for years before squash appeared on the scene and which was never played outside the US. The two games were played in courts which had nearly similar dimensions. The figures for squash tennis were 32 feet 6 inches long by 17 feet wide. Those for squash racquets were 32 feet long by 18 feet 6 inches wide. The main difference in the two games were provided by the speed of the ball, and by the balls themselves. The squash tennis ball which weighs just under two ounces is nearly twice as heavy as the squash ball. It is also larger at 2 9/16 inches in diameter compared to

69

the squash ball whose diameter was only 1 ¾ inches. The squash tennis ball is highly inflated to a pressure of 45 to 50 pounds per square inch. The net result of these dimensions is that the squash tennis ball was much faster than the squash ball. As Allison Danzig has it: "In squash tennis the speed is in the ball; in squash racquets it is in the players' legs".

The squash tennis stronghold was New York but in 1914 the New York Racquet and Tennis Club which had two squash tennis courts, switched to squash racquets, using the slower ball and lighter racquets but playing in the same courts. Other clubs followed the lead of the Racquet and Tennis Club and from then on squash tennis declined just as squash racquets gained in popularity. Although speed is part of the American way of life, the speed of the ball in squash tennis which increased with the years proved too much for the average player.

It is admitted that squash started in England some 50 years before it reached the US. There are no records to show how the game crossed the Atlantic. There is an apocryphal tale that an eminent divine who lived near Detroit went to stay with a friend in Canada and was delighted with the squash court at his host's house. Wanting to import the game to the US our divine went down one night to measure the court, but his friend's hospitality had made him careless and he returned to Detroit with the wrong measurements, which is supposed to account for the American court being narrower than the courts in the rest of the world. But, if true, this must have been sometime late in the last century when there were no standard measurements laid down anywhere in the world.

A curious difference between the American and British game lies in the spelling. In England and indeed in the rest of the world the spelling of 'rackets' is preferred. But in the early days of rackets and squash in England the word was frequently spelt with a 'Q'. In America they have remained faithful to the 'Q' variety. It has been said that the Americans wanted to be quite certain that there should be no connection with the 'CK' variety of the word, commonly used in America and defined in a dictionary as 'an organised criminal activity of the underworld!'

We have seen that Philadelphia was the spriritual home of squash in the US. In Boston the game had a slightly different origin. In 1888 the Boston Athletic Association was opened and therein a small court was built for the purpose of playing Rugby Fives, one of the three Fives games still played to a certain extent in England, the others being Eton Fives and Winchester Fives. In these games the small ball is hit with the hand instead of a racket. The game as played in Boston was too strenuous for the average player and soon was being played with a lawn tennis ball and a bat. Thus squash tennis came to Boston. Later squash tennis courts were added to this Boston Athletic Association which were larger than a fives court. The game proved a success and led to the formation of the Massachusetts Squash Association in 1902.

Wood was used for all four walls of these courts. In 1905 however a member of the Boston Tennis and Racquets Club visited Philadelphia and there discovered squash racquets. He brought back with him the long handled racquet and soft ball. The game was then tried out in the squash tennis courts and found so much favour that it was presented to the Board of Directors of the Massachusetts Squash Association. The Board were impressed with the possibilities of the game and decided to adopt it and so the Boston clubs began the switch from squash tennis to squash racquets. No great change was made in the courts, the only differences being the height of the telltale, the service line on the front wall and the floor markings.

From the time of the 1914-18 War the greatest centre of squash in the USA was Harvard University. Soon after 1924 the racquet and squash tennis courts were converted into squash courts and by 1929 the University sported 30 courts, a figure which has now grown considerably.

Reference has already been made to the squash court erected in New York at the 43rd Street Clubhouse of the Racquet and Tennis Club. This was built about 1891 and was originally called a fives court. For some reason this court, which was built of cement, was never used and squash was not played in New York until long after it was flourishing in Philadelphia and Boston. Squash Tennis was deeply entrenched in the city. Two squash tennis courts were built at the Racquets and Tennis Club shortly after opening its clubhouse in 43rd Street. It was not until 1914 that the Club switched over in these courts from squash tennis to squash racquets, using the slower ball and lighter racquet. Other clubs in the district soon followed the lead of the Racquet and Tennis Club. During the 1914-18 War the University Club in New York started to build two squash tennis courts but they were finished off with glazed cement so that they could be used for squash racquets. Two more courts for squash racquets were built by the University Club which then became the headquarters of the game in New York.

The Metropolitan Squash Racquets Association was formed in 1924, one of the objects of which was to arrange inter club matches but it was not until 1928 that a metropolitan league was formed. Squash racquets in New York received a fillip from the number of Harvard graduates who came to work in the city and the visit of the first British team in 1924 acted as a further boost. In 1923 the Metropolitan Championships were inaugurated at the University Club but with the founding of the Metropolitan Open in 1969 the title was changed to The Metropolitan 'A'.

Reference has been made to the Racquet and Tennis Club in New York which had its premises in 43rd Street. In 1918 this club moved into Park Avenue where its magnificent building still stands. In the move, squash tennis was finally abandoned and in its place were constructed four squash racquets courts, and it was here that the first national championship to be held in New York took place in 1929. It was this event which finally proved that New York was no longer the stronghold of squash tennis and had taken its place as one of the chief centres of squash racquets in America.

The first national amateur championship was held in Philadelphia in 1907 and in the following year the team championship was started. Apart from three occasions when the Nationals, as The Amateur Championship came to be known, were held in Boston, every Championship up to 1923 was held in Philadelphia which might be described as the cradle of American squash. Since 1923 a large number of cities have hosted the Championship. Only once — in 1924 — has the Championship been won by a player not resident in America. In that year the winner was Gerald Robarts, a member of the British team touring the US at that time. Anil Nayar, an Indian, won in 1969 and 1970. Although brought up on the British game (he became British junior champion in 1965), he lived in the US while an undergraduate at Harvard and later lived in Boston. In recent years the Canadians have figured prominently and Colin Adair from Montreal won the Championship in 1968 and 1971. Michael Desaulniers, another Canadian won in 1978.

In 1954 the first US Open Championship was held in New York. Because the tournament was scheduled for completion in one weekend the entries were limited to 20. All the leading American professionals and amateurs entered, but chief interest centred on the first appearance in competitive squash in America of Hashim Khan and Mahmoud Karim. Neither of these two great players took the trouble to acclimatise themselves to the American game before the start of the Championship and both were beaten by Henri Salaun who won the Nationals in the same year. In the final Salaun won the final rally at 14-all, to inflict on Hashim his first defeat in competition play for many years. In the next year Hashim was forced by injury to retire but thereafter the Championship became almost a Pakistani preserve, Americans winning it on only two occasions between 1956 and 1974. In 1965 the Championship was amalgamated with the Canadian Open Championship and renamed the North American Open Championship.

ANGLO-AMERICAN COMPETITION

The story of Anglo-American competition commenced with the receipt by the Tennis and Rackets Association of a letter in March 1923 from Mr W. S. Greening one of the leading players in Toronto, Canada inviting a British team to visit America early in 1924 to play a series of matches against club teams in the United States and Canada and to take part in the Lapham Trophy competition which had been started in 1922 when Henry G. Lapham offered a cup bearing his name for annual competition between the US and Canada. With a view to extending the scope of international competition the national associations of the two American countries decided that the rules of the Trophy could be widened to include a British team when playing in America. The British response was favourable and at a meeting of the Representatives Committee held in July attended by E. M. Hinkle, captain of Harvard University team and who was visiting England, further details were agreed.

This of course was long before the days of a regular selection committee and those who were picked for the team would have to pay their own way to America and back. Finance as well as form therefore entered into it and it was ordered that a notice should be put up in all the clubs and squash courts asking members who were able to go to put their names down for selection.

Meanwhile preparations for the British visit went on apace in America. It was arranged that the US Championships should be held in Boston a week before the Lapham Trophy contest which was to be held in Philadelphia, and the Canadians arranged to have their championships delayed from January until February in order that the British team could compete in them.

Realising that the absence of financial support might make it impossible for some otherwise suitable players to go to America, the Representatives Committee suggested that a subscription should be started to raise financial assistance for those in need of it, but the T & RA would have none of it and passed a resolution that the tour should be under its auspices on the understanding that the members of the team paid their own expenses, and that all the arrangements should be placed in the hands of the squash committee. Evidently the T & RA were getting worried that control of the game was being grasped by the Representatives Committee and that any financial assistance to members of the team would be against the spirit of amateur play!

The British team which eventually went to America consisted of S. M. Toyne, Dr T. Drysdale, Col W. F. Bassett, W. D. MacPherson and Captain Gerald Robarts. The tour was a great success for the British, playing the unfamiliar American game. England came second in the Lapham Trophy matches with 6 wins to the US 7½, with Canada a long way behind at 1½. Gerald Robarts won both the US and the Canadian titles.

It was during this tour that discussions took place for the first time on the differences between the two games. On their return to England Sam Toyne and Dr Drysdale reported on this to the Representatives Committee who appointed the inevitable sub-committee to go into the matter thoroughly. It is of interest that all this was being done by the Representatives Committee and not by the T & RA.

The sub-committee reported that the rules of rackets should be taken as the rules of squash with certain proposed alterations and these were then to be delivered to the T & RA.

The one concrete suggestion which came from the USA as a means of bringing the two games closer together was the lowering of the tin, and in 1924 the Representatives Committee asked all clubs to experiment with a lower tin, but this the clubs were reported as unwilling to do.

The success of the British tour in America had resulted in an invitation to the US and Canadian Associations to send a team to England. The original invitation was for the tour to embrace the Amateur championship in December but the Americans were unable to raise a team at that time.

It was then suggested that the Amateur Championship should be postponed until mid-January if by so doing the Americans would be able to send their team over.

The second British visit to America was the result of an invitation received in August 1926 to make a tour from the middle of January 1927 to the end of February, which times included the sea trips. No less than twelve players were selected. This was a pretty hefty order and it was thought wise to cable the USSA Committee to enquire if this was too many! But the Americans appeared unmoved and accepted the lot.

Over the years international transatlantic competition has been severely restricted by the differences in the American and British versions of the game. It is an acknowledged fact that it is easier to transfer from the British to the American game than vice-versa. Touring teams cannot normally spend sufficient time to become acclimatised to the other game. After the reconstruction of the squash courts at the RAC in London in 1947, there was one — the only one in fact — American sized court in England. This court also had American court markings and the Committee were generous in permitting teams preparing to cross the Atlantic to practice in this court.

But before the war successful attempts were made to promote transatlantic tours, and the first British team to play in America, as already stated, arrived in New York early in 1924. The team was a private one, for this was before the formation of the SRA. The captain was S. M. Toyne and the others to sail with him were W. F. Basset, Dr T. Drysdale and Capt G. Robarts. All are now dead, but in America they were able to recruit W. D. MacPherson who won the Amateur Championships in that year and was at that time studying at Harvard University. The team had hoped to make use of another player as a reserve who had crossed over with them. Unfortunately he was arrested on his arrival in New York as the result of a domestic wrangle with his wife in England. In spite of the fact that, with the exception of MacPherson, all the players were over the age of 40, the team stood up remarkably well to eighteen days of hard matches, travelling and the usual American super-hospitality and won nine of their eleven matches, being defeated only by the US national team (by one game) and by Boston. What is more Gerald Robarts won the US and Canadian Championships. In all Robarts played 17 matches in 19 days and won them all — a magnigicient record for a man in his forty sixth year. He was never able to win the British Amateur Championship, being beaten either by T. O. Jameson or W. D. MacPherson.

Mention may be made here of the Lapham Trophy, in which the 1924 British team were invited to compete. In 1922 Henry G. Lapham offered a cup bearing his name for annual competition between the US and Canada, held alternately in each country. The deed of gift specified that it was to be a perpetual trophy and that the competition was to be called the "International Squash Rackets Championship". Teams were to consist of not less than five nor more than fifteen players, usually the latter. In 1924 the British team easily defeated the Canadians but was beaten 3-2 by the US team, Toyne, Drysdale and Basset losing, while Robarts and MacPherson won.

In 1925 the US sent a weak team to England which contained none of the previous years victorious team in the International match. Britain were at full strength and the unfortunate Americans did not win a game, much less a tie.

In 1927 the second International team visited the States and Canada. Again they were invited to play in the Lapham Trophy and this time were successful. The team drew three matches all with the US but won the trophy by reason of a better result than the US against Canada. The star player of the British team was Capt Victor Cazalet, four times winner of the Amateur Championship in England. He just failed to win the US Championship but in the final of the Canadian Championship, against R. S. Wright of Chicago, played superb squash to win by the astonishing score of 17-18, 17-18, 17-16, 15-11, 17-16. Wright subsequently spent some time in England and played in the Amateur Championship, and on two occasions reached the semi-final. In addition to Cazalet the team consisted of Col Basset, a veteran from the previous team and in his forty-eighth year, P. de L. Cazenove, G. S. Incledon-Webber, Capt G. N. Scott-Chad and F. M. Strawson. This team was a more ambitious affair than the first, the team being away from England for two months. The final tally was: played 20, won 15, drawn 2, lost 3.

The next British mens team to visit America was the Jesters in 1934. The team contained six players, one of whom was H. T. H. Drysdale whose father had been a member of Sam Toyne's team in 1924. As this was a club side they were not invited to play in the Lapham Trophy, but the Canadian Championship final was fought out by two members of the team, Edward Snell and John Gillies, and won by Snell. In the last match of the tour Snell had a fine victory over Beekman Pool the reigning US Amateur Champion.

Cambridge University sent teams to tour America in 1938 and 1952 with considerable success and Yale University has toured the UK on more than one occasion since the war. The reason that there has not been more transatlantic travel is certainly due to the expense of the fares, and this applies more to British than American teams.

If competition between the two continents has been severely limited as far as the men are concerned, the same cannot be said of the women. In 1933 the first British Women's team landed in New York and on February 22 the International match series between the two countries was commenced at the Sleepy Hollow Club and was won by the British 4-1. At the dinner following the match the British Captain, Mrs G. Bryans-Wolfe and Miss S. Noel announced that they were donating the Wolfe-Noel Cup for competition between the two countries. The Great Britain team have won three times in America and have never been remotely threatened in matches in this country. Up to and including 1968 the tally was GB 11, USA 5.

THE AMERICAN AND THE INTERNATIONAL GAME

Much has been written as well as said about the difference between the 'British' and American games of squash. The chief differences are three in number:

        a. Court dimension;
        b. The Ball;
        c. The Scoring.

Obviously the game came to America from England and in the latter years of the 19th century there were no standard court measurements in England so that a person introducing squash to America could have picked up one of a variety of court dimensions. While there is some evidence that squash came to the USA from England via Canada the game, once it had taken root in both transatlantic countries, progressed more rapidly in the USA. In Canada, while the early court dimensions were narrower than those which came to be standardised later in England, the ball was a soft one and the scoring was English rather than American. It was not until after the 1914-18 War that Canada adopted the hard ball and the American scoring, both of which were imported from the USA.

Efforts have been made from time to time to bring the two games together. The chief stumbling block has always been the ball. The American sized courts now represent more than 40% of the total number of courts in the world and it is universally recognised that nothing can be done about this, nor is the difference in dimension, nor the court markings an outstanding bar to the adoption of a universal game.

The ball question however is vital and is undoubtedly the main stumbling block. The hard American ball may well have been imported from England where there were, even up to 1922, a wide variety of balls used, some hard, some soft, some large, some small.

The American ball is larger, heavier and has a higher bounce than the British ball.

From time to time the question of a compromise ball has been considered but it was not until 1976 that the 70 + ball was produced and sold by the West Company, ball manufacturers in the USA. This ball is the same size as the British or International ball but harder, although not as hard as the American ball. It has been well received in America and in 1977 was adopted as the official ball of the USSRA.

The main difference in the scoring is that in the International game the player can only score a point if he is serving whereas in American scoring a point is scored at the end of every rally. Also in International scoring a game is nine points whereas in America the game is 15.

The merits of the two methods have been hotly debated for many years and in 1954 the SRA appointed a sub-committee "to consider what steps, if any, can usefully be taken to bring the British and American forms of the game closer together". The committee reported that nothing could be done about the sizes of the courts, that the possibility of an intermediate ball should be investigated, but that all clubs in England should be asked to experiment with American scoring. Only 20% of the clubs volunteered to try the experiment and of those who did there was a majority of seven to one against any change. In answer to the questions "Did you enjoy the game more?" the majority who enjoyed it less was ten to one. How much of this antagonism to the American game was due to the innate conservatism of the British is hard to determine, but the figures were sufficiently conclusive to kill any further attempts to bring the games together until 1971 when Mr Stewart Brauns jr, the President of the USSRA proposed to the ISRF the adoption of a compromise game with the Australian type ball and American scoring. The ISRF asked its members to try out the suggestion but, judging from the small number of replies, the squash world was not interested.

Interesting developments are however taking place in America — chiefly in Canada where the international or soft ball game is making great strides. Ever since the late sixties, Dr Quentin Hyder, an English psychologist practising in New York organised annually in April a tournament played under International rules and with Australian balls, but in American courts. In both the USA and Canada summer leagues were held under the same conditions. The hard American ball becomes almost unplayable in the heat of the American summer. Since 1975 the International game has made such strides in Canada that there is now a national soft ball championship played annually and the soft ball game is now played to an increasing extent all the year round.

The holding of the International Championships in Canada in 1977 gave a tremendous impetus to the 'soft ball' game in that country and it does appear that the American game is being squeezed out as far as Canada is concerned. In the USA however the 'hard ball' game is fighting hard — and so far successfully — against the soft ball variety. But there, a new threat to squash has been posed by the success of a new game — racquetball — particularly in the West. This is the easiest of all racket games and is supposed to be played in a court using the four walls, the floor and the roof. The players use a short handled racket and a rubber ball with a high bounce and about the size of a tennis ball. While one can learn to hit this ball and learn the simple rules more easily than at squash the general feeling is that the game is too easy and that it may well turn out to be a good recruiting counter for squash. While a certain number of racquet ball courts have been built in the USA and a few in Canada the game is usually played on squash courts and is not in the long term looked upon as a major threat to squash. It has also been introduced with modifications into England and Australia.

CHAPTER VI

EQUIPMENT AND THE COURT

THE RACKET

*T*HERE CAN be no doubt that the Harrow schoolboys first hit that soft ball with the racket which they were waiting to use on the rackets court. It is probable that as the game developed they used the same racket with the end sawn off to make it easier to wield in the narrower confines of the 'squash court'. Even the records of Grays of Cambridge are curiously silent on the question of when rackets for the game of squash were first manufactured by the firm. H. J. Gray, the rackets professional at St Johns College, Cambridge, founded the firm in 1855. Yet it was not until the closing years of the last century that there is any record in the firm of squash rackets. These had flat tops as did lawn tennis rackets of that day. It must be remembered that the early rackets were much more slender than they are today, which made it easier for them to be used for squash. Curiously the weight of squash rackets has in recent years tended to increase. In the nineteen thirties it averaged at between 7¾ to 8 oz (although Charles Arnold used a 6¾ oz racket). Today the weight is between 8 and 8½ oz. For many years Grays made the frames and sold them to the professionals who strung them with gut. Sheep's gut is the commonest used. The well known advertisement of two cats talking — "My father's in that racket" — is probably a myth. There were not that number of cats about anyway! The wooden frames were steam bent until the thirties when laminating came into fashion.

While Grays were first in the field to make squash rackets, the increasing popularity of the game after World War I led to a rash of racket makers and by the middle thirties there were at least 13 companies engaged in this work. The practise of using the name of a leading player to popularise a racket was well established in the thirties.

Jim Dear was employed by Grays before he went to Queens Club and gave his name to Grays rackets for many years. Arnold and Butcher were other champions associated with racket making firms which no longer exist.

In 1908 squash rackets were made at the Searle Street, Cambridge factory of Grays and were solid rendered ash, hand made. At that time two men were employed on racquet production turning out between 20 and 24 racquets per week, while in 1912 manufacture was doubled by the employment of two more men. By 1932 production had been stepped up to nearly 100 per week. Retail price was 10/6d each. The prowess of the members of the Grays family at rackets led to the founding of the racket making firm of that name, and Grays had a long lead over any other firms when it came to the manufacture of rackets — it is only Grays who nowadays still use the old spelling of racquets. It was a small and natural step to the manufacture of squash rackets. Compared with Grays, Dunlop came into the squash rackets production comparatively late — about the early thirties. Their chief factory is at Waltham Abbey, Hertfordshire.

In recent years most of the racket frames have been made in the East — Taiwan and Pakistan chiefly. The great squash boom caught the racket manufacturers unprepared and it was only in 1976 that the production of rackets began to catch up with the demand.

Attempts have been made from time to time to market squash rackets with a soft metal head frame but the International Squash Rackets Federation has refused to bow to commercial pressure, having decided that rackets of this type are dangerous and so should be declared illegal.

THE BALL

The literature of all ball games is lamentably small and hence we know all too little about how the various court games were played in the middle ages and with what type of ball. We do know that the ball which was used for hand ball was softer than the ball used for racket games.

In the 18th century real tennis balls were made of strips of cloth rolled together and stitched. Later the exterior was of leather and stuffed with wool, feathers or hair. The harder type of ball which bounced higher off the floor became the acknowledged ball for rackets.

But what of the ball originally used for squash? We do know that it was not a rackets ball which would have been far too fast for the small

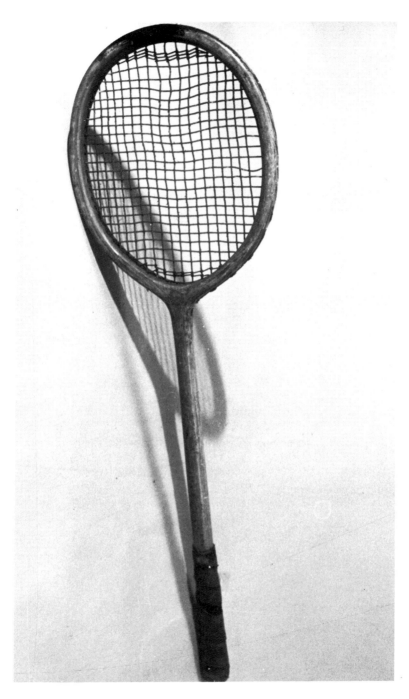

The early squash racket — solid rendered ash, hand-made by Grays.

confines of a squash court. Besides we are told that the name of the game originated from the 'squashy' sound made by the ball on impact with the wall, very different from the hard 'plop' of a rackets ball. Most probably it was an ordinary child's rubber ball. While the size and shape of the racket has remained comparatively stable, the same cannot be said of the ball. There were wide variations in the size, hardness and even colour of the squash ball. Trial and error led to certain balls being chosen as best suited to a court and when it came to championship play, the ball chosen depended on the court — and its size. But the Womens Championship frequently changed their ball. In 1925, the RAC standard ball was used, in 1926 the Gradidge standard 'nigger' and in 1927 the Wisden Standard. The Tennis and Rackets Association which nursed the infant squash for many years laid down a specification for squash balls and it is curious that for some years after the formation of the Squash Rackets Association, the T&RA continued to mark authorised balls. From the plethora of balls used in championships and matches, by 1930 the Silvertown ball came to be recognised as the best. During the 1939-45 War the East London factory of the East India Gutta Percha Company which made the Silvertown ball was destroyed by enemy action. It has always been said that the secret of the mix was also destroyed. Certain it is that the Silvertown ball was never made again and in its place there remained Dunlops, who were the sole ball manufacturers for many years in England.

In modern times the success or failure of a ball has been largely dependent on its lasting capabilities. There was one year in the mid-sixties when one was lucky to end a match with the same ball with which it had been started. The fault here was corrected but even now, in the mid-seventies, balls have an infuriating habit of breaking — often at some crisis in a match. Times is wasted and the more tired of the players gets an undeserved time bonus while the substitute ball is warmed up.

Until recently it has been almost impossible to prevent the walls of the court from being marked by the ball. Painting the walls certainly made cleaning easier but it also had the disadvantage of increasing the danger of sweating walls. Now non-marking balls have appeared on the market which has largely got over this difficulty.

THE COURT

The close relationship between rackets and squash is no better exemplified than by the similarity between the court markings of the two games. But when one comes to compare the actual court one must remember that in the early days squash was played in any rectangular "room". The earliest illustration of the game being played showed only two walls, the front and right hand side, but this game was played in ad hoc conditions making use of what was at that time available. When squash courts started to be built from scratch the opportunity was taken to build four walls, as in rackets, and the appearance of the court, not to mention the lines on the court floor, gave rise to the name "mini-rackets" by which squash was frequently known in those days.

It should be remembered that in England no authoritative dimensions of a squash court were laid down until the game had been played for over 70 years, these were the dimensions laid down by a sub-committee of the Tennis and Rackets Association in 1922, seven years before the SRA was formed. By that time, a large number of courts had been built in various parts of the world, apart from England (see Chapter V) and there was a wide variety in the sizes of the court. Even in 1922, when the first Amateur Championship was played in London, the organisers had a choice of different sized courts from which to select the venue of the championship. But whatever the size or composition of the court, the special relationship with rackets has kept the floor markings similar apart from the size of the court.

Next let us consider the floor. In that two sided court where squash was first played, the floor was of asphalt. But when courts were first built specially for the game, the walls and floor were made of wood, probably to save the expense of asphalt, and until quite recent times this was the material of which courts were constructed in America. This made the game extremely noisy. There are still in use in this country a number of wooden courts, and I speak as one who has played in them. Gradually the courts came to be built with bricks faced with a hard composition material, normally called plaster, and this became the standard method of construction.

The main drawback of walls made in this way has been the tendency to sweat in certain atmospheric conditions, resulting in a thin film of moisture condensing on the walls, and sometimes even on the floor which caused the balls to skid even to the point of making the court unplayable. More recently courts have been erected with painted concrete slabs as walls which has proved effective in reducing sweating. Before the War one could buy portable wooden courts and about 20 years ago there were courts on sale with foldable side walls of wood which could be fitted into a gymnasium.

The floor of the court is normally made up of wooden slats, and for many years maple was advocated, but recently other and cheaper woods have been found satisfactory as well. When one remembers that for many years courts were built either singly or at most in pairs at country houses, where they were not often used, or in schools not overburdened with money, it was necessary to use cheap materials which is why asphalt and concrete were not used, quite apart from the fact that wooden floors, nowadays sprung, are kinder on the feet. But composition floors were used at Lancing College, which has an outstanding record for the game among public schools, and whether the success of those who learnt their squash there had anything to do with the composition of the floor is an arguable point.

In the early days natural lighting through glass panels in the roof provided sufficient illumination but when lights hanging from the roof were introduced it frequently happened that rain seeped through imperfect joints in the panels. Many courts had iron girders spanning the roof which collected moisture through condensation. This became oxidized and fell through to the floor, staining the wooden slats a dark colour. As squash was mainly an evening exercise natural lighting became less important and has disappeared from more recently built courts. Tungsten lighting gave way to fluorescent lighting which being cheaper became popular and is extensively used nowadays.

RULES OF THE GAME

Nowhere were the haphazard beginnings of squash better shown than in the Rules of the Game. In the absence of a governing body the Tennis and Rackets Association which itself was not founded until 1907 'looked after' the growing game of squash through the Squash Rackets Committee of that body. Laws of Squash Rackets were laid down in 1920 and these included standard dimensions for a squash court. Although the Squash Rackets Association had been formed in December 1928, the game was played for some time after that date under rules approved by the Tennis and Rackets Assciation in July 1930, in which year the title was changed to "The Rules of Squash Rackets".

The Rules themselves naturally bore a close resemblance to the Rules of Rackets, and up to 1926 a game consisted of up to 15 points. It was in that year that the present scoring of nine points came into being. As the game developed and became more competitive it became necessary to deal with an increasing number of situations in play, and this aspect of the game has continued up to the present day. The Laws, up to 1930 covered a mere 1,200 words, but in that year the number of words jumped to 2,100. Today it is nearly 3,000.

With two players running around at speed in a confined space it was necessary to lay down a code of conduct to deal with the problem of getting out of each other's way. "Rule 17 — Fair View" (Law 24 under the old Laws) has been the most controversial rule which successive committees of both the SRA and the ISRF have tried to better over the years. Until after the 1939/45 War the rule stated that each player must get out of the way as much as possible and if players did not do any of the three things laid down as pre requisites, the referee was empowered "on appeal, or without waiting for an appeal, allow a Let, or a stroke to his opponent, if in his opinion such is a fair decision considering all the circumstances, and in accordance with what would probably have happened had there been no such interference". This wording was utterly weak especially when dealing with probabilities. For some years after the War few matches had more than one official in charge, and if he were a professional it was unlikely that he would have the courage, when dealing with amateur players, to exert the ultimate penalty of allowing a stroke against the offending player.

Players who did not bother to get out of the way, having made a stroke, were called baulkers, and from the dawn of competitive squash there have been baulkers. Charles Read, in his book on the game, simply advised his pupils to refuse to play opponents who offended in this manner, and while this was good advice when dealing with friendly games, it did not cover competition in match play. Matters came to a head in the Army Championships in 1946/7 when two senior officers, both well known to be baulkers, clashed in the quarter-finals. The four games played resulted in 67 lets in addition to a great deal of ill feeling. The Hon Secretary of the Professionals Committee (D. G. Butcher) wrote officially on behalf of his Committee to the SRA and claimed that unless something was done to check the increasing habit of baulking, the game would be ruined. The Executive Committee of the SRA took the easy way out and simply told the Chairman of the Rules sub-committee to 'do something'. Borrowing from the American rules, the SRA eventually gave some teeth to the old rule by the addition of: "If in the opinion of the referee the failure to comply with the provisions of this rule is unnecessary, he shall immediately stop play and award a stroke to the offending player's opponent". Moreover, additional power was given to the referee in the following Note:

"a. The practice of impeding an opponent's strokes by crowding or by obscuring his view is highly detrimental to the game and referees should have no hestitation in enforcing the final paragraph of this rule.

b. The words 'interfering with . . . him in getting to . . . the ball' must be interpreted so as to include the case of a player's having to wait for an excessive swing of his opponent's racket".

This was by no means the end of the matter. Rather was it the beginning of a controversy which has continued to this day. Professionals who normally combined the duties of referee and marker were for years loth to award what came to be known as penalty points (although it may be pointed out that this name is not mentioned in the rule itself). They argued that they depended for their livelihood on the goodwill of amateurs, which would be lost if the professional penalised them in this way. It was also argued that the rule dealt with deliberate interference but the SRA were quick to point out that 'deliberate' was an attitude of mind and it was not possible to know what was in the mind of a player — hence the word, carefully chosen, was 'unnecessary'. Slowly the squash world began to realise that here was a rule which if applied would cure the evil of the persistent baulker. For it is only the persistent wrongdoer to which the rule should apply. In the modern game it has come to be recognised that interference is sometimes accidental, but the penalty point should nevertheless be given, without any stigma of unfairness attaching to the offender.

While no rule has been so persistently examined or amended as Rule 17, the greater rewards for winning have led to the introduction of new rules to deal with unfair practices. An example of this is the power given to the referee to award a game to the opponent of any player who persists, after due warning in delaying play in order to recover his wind or for any other reason. This was passed in 1960 in which year the provision for umpires was abolished. This was a rule borrowed from the Laws of Rackets under which provision was made for two umpires to assist the referee. Fortunately this part of the rule was permissive and not obligatory. Umpires were occasionally used in international matches before the War but by 1960 had died a natural death years before. The words 'cut' and 'short' which were supposed to be used by the marker, and which were also a hangover from rackets, also disappeared in this year.

When the ISRF was formed in 1967 it naturally took over from the SRA the responsibility for the rules of the game. In 1971 a Rules Interpretation sub-committee was appointed consisting of three of the ablest experts on the rules — R. B. Hawkey (GB), V. N. Hunt (Australia) and K. Jarvis (South Africa). The sub-committee from time to time put forward amendments to the Rules but with distances making meetings impossible it was sometimes difficult to get agreement between members of the sub-committee. A new draft of the Rules based largely on the recommendations of the sub-committee (by which time J. Roy (South Africa) had succeeded K. Jarvis) was finally issued by the ISRF late in 1976 to come into operation in January 1977.

While it is virtually impossible to play a game of rackets without a marker, this did not apply to squash and in the days before there were organised competitions, the players kept the score and if in the course of play obstruction occurred, a request for a let was automatically acceded to by the opponent. When the Bath Club Cup was commenced in 1922, the professional at the home team's club marked and refereed the games but as competitive squash expanded, there were many matches where no professional was available and these were either marked by members of the teams involved, or by the players themselves. But the introduction of 'penalty points' created a new situation. It was difficult for the players themselves to decide whether a request for a let should result in a let or a harsher penalty. The professionals were none too happy at having to shoulder the increased responsibilities and for a long time refused to award penalty points. Their argument was that as they were dependent for their living on the goodwill of the amateurs, it was not fair to risk antagonising the amateurs by awarding points against them. But gradually the pros began to see the advantages of the new rule, and to use it as it should be used. It must be admitted that the application of the new rule demanded a degree of intelligence as well as of concentration and its introduction made the marking of matches unpopular with a large number of players, particularly top class amateurs.

The coaching courses organised by the SRA included some lectures on marking and refereeing but it was not until 1971 that the Director of Coaching began a scheme of courses and examinations whereby would-be referees and markers were lectured on the Rules and the correct method of administering them, and subsequently examined. In 1972 25 amateur referees had been awarded the SRA Certificate. In 1975 a classification system was introduced for the top referees and markers. Professionals came into the scheme in 1974 and by 1976 268 certificates had been awarded to players in the British Isles. These included 19 professionals and 16 women. The SRA was asked to send a number of referees and markers to Karachi to officiate at the two big tournaments held there in 1976. In spite of the tremendous efforts of Dick Hawkey and the National Coaches it must be admitted that at the chief Championship events in the 1976/7 season there was considerable inconsistency in the referees interpretation of Rule 17, and the players and the media were not slow to voice their dissatisfaction. SRA certified referees are in great demand.

CHAPTER VII

THE GREATS
OF THE GAME

THE KHAN SAGA

THERE CAN seldom have been a game at which so many of the top performers in the world were closely related and came from a small part of one country. The Khan dynasty in Pakistan has produced at least five world champions and while most of these are now past their best, the new generation of Pakistani professionals are distantly connected.

In considering the families involved, it is important to remember that Khan is a sort of tribal name, and the organisers of squash tournaments and their programmes merely confuse the subject when they refer to A. Khan or M. Khan. It is the first name which is the important one and should always be printed in full. Even when this is done there can arise difficulties as when considering Mohibullah; is one referring to the son of Safirullah or the much younger runner-up in the World Championship in 1976?

Most members of the family come from Nawekille, a village one mile from Peshawar, a city in what was the hilly North-West Frontier Province of India and is now Pakistan. There are two main families involved, the descendants of Rehmatullah, the Imam or prayer leader of Peshawar and those of Muhammed Ali. They became related by marriage. Yet the most famous squash players, Hashim and his brother Azam were not descendants of either of the two named above. It was Hashim's sister who married Safirullah who was a descendant of Rehmatullah, and this brought Hashim and his brother into the family. These two were the sons of one Abdullah who was no more than a competent performer, and whose main occuptation was Head Butler at the Officers Club at Peshawar. He died in an accident in 1927 when Hashim was still a child and the boy was looked after by Majeed Khan, son of Rehmatullah, who was principal marker at the Peshawar Club. Majeed is considered the grandfather of squash and rackets in India and ran a school for markers. Anyone wanting a marker applied to Majeed who would send one of his pupils. It was in this way that both Hashim and, later, Azam obtained their first appointments. Majeed's game as a player was mainly at rackets — he was fairly old when squash was introduced to the Peshawar Club where he was rackets professional for sixty-five years, having started there as a ball boy. His eldest son, Ismatullah was marker to the Viceroy before joining his father at Peshawar, and the young Hashim obtained valuable coaching from him as he relates in his entertaining book, 'Squash Rackets' by Hashim Khan (Souvenir Press). Safirullah, who was born in 1918 is still the marker at the Sind Club, Karachi, and his son, Mohibullah succeeded Azam as British Open Champion in 1962. He is now resident in the USA.

The head of the other great squash family in Pakistan was Muhammad Ali. One of his sons Said Ali was a well known rackets and squash professional and played in the All India Professional Championship in 1944, aged 60. He was the father of Abdul Bari who became the first Pakistani professional to obtain employment in England and was professional at the Junior Carlton Club, London from 1952 until his untimely death two years later at the early age of 33.

Muhammed Ali's daughter married a man of property and their son Faizullah Khan married a daughter of Majeed Khan, which thereby made him a brother-in-law of Hashim and Azam. Their eldest son, Nazrullah Khan, born in 1920, was a fine player but is better known as the finest teacher of the game in England. He succeeded his cousin Bari at the Junior Carlton Club and was later at the Lansdowne Club and the Edgbaston-Priory Club in Birmingham. His younger brother Roshan Khan has been for many years chief coach to the Pakistan Navy. He was probably the finest stroke player of all the Khans and visited England annually for the Championships in the fifties. Hashim was grooming Azam, 11 years his junior to succeed him as Open Champion and looked upon Roshan as a threat to his plans. In 1957 Roshan reached the final of the Open Championship in London and faced Hashim, whose legs had been giving him trouble — and who should blame them after the terrible hammering their owner had subjected them to over the years! Hashim won the first game but thereafter Roshan ran the champion round the court mercilessly and won the next three games with increasing ease. This was Roshan's only win in the Open Championship. He suffered from a recurrent knee injury which forced him to withdraw from the Open in the following

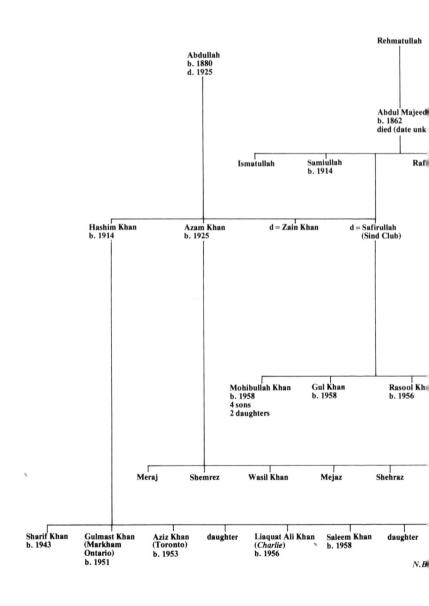

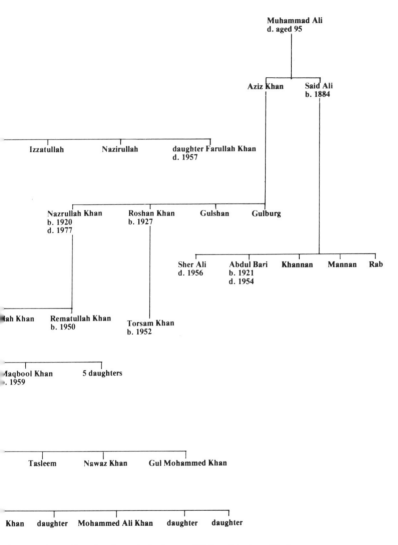

...ths and deaths are given where known in the absence of births and deaths certificates.

91

year and though in 1960 he again reached the final against Azam, his knee gave way again and he scored only one point in the match. Although Rashan used to go on to the USA for the rich pickings to be obtained from exhibition matches, unlike his cousin Hashim, he did not settle there. Hashim, all the time he was winning his championships outside Pakistan was still coach to the Air Force in Pakistan, but in 1960 he decided to quit the English game and accepted a professional appointment in Detroit, USA. Meanwhile, Azam with some help from his brother, took over the New Grampians Squash Club in West London and is still the resident proprietor and professional. He injured his Achilles tendon in 1962 and although he made a good recovery, never played competitively again, thus ending at 37 a career which could have gone on for many years. He frequently proved, in playing friendly games, and while later coaching Jonah Barrington, that he had lost none of his old skill, but with four Open Championships under his belt he probably thought that he had done enough for glory and it was unthinkable that he should try and beat the record of seven Open Championships set up by his elder brother.

In the intervals of playing squash, both Hashim and Azam sired many children — Hashim twelve and Azam nine. Hashim's eldest, Sharif Khan who was educated at the English public school Millfield where he was given a sports scholarship, eventually decided to follow in his father's footsteps in America. He had started promisingly at English squash by winning the Drysdale Cup (Junior Championship) in 1963 but then left for America where he became the greatest player, winning the Open Championship there so far nine times. It is interesting to record that since 1955 Pakistanis have won this Championship 17 times out of 21. Azam and Roshan are the only winners who are not resident professionals in America. In addition to Sharif, two other sons of Hashim, Gulmast and Aziz are also professionals, but of Azam's children, who are of course much younger, only Wasil has shown promise. Two sons of Nazrullah, Amanullah (b. 1948) and Rematullah (b. 1950) have been successful as professionals in England while Roshan's son Torsam competes regularly in the professional events of the International game.

Hashim has had honours heaped upon him in his native country and in 1976 the Pakistan International Airways presented a trophy named after him for a team event which attracted the world's best players to Karachi. The event was a great success in spite of the heat, and the then lack of air conditioning. Hashim and others of the Khans were brought back to Pakistan from all over the world to share in the praises showered upon one of Pakistan's greatest sons.

BIOGRAPHIES

IBRAHIM AMIN (1934-   )

When Ibrahim Amin arrived in England in December 1955 he was an unknown player. Unseeded, he won the Amateur Championship and at 21 years of age was then the youngest player to do so since Amr Bey. The fact that in the final he survived two match points only emphasises his precocious coolness in a crisis. Then came Suez and he was forced to miss the 1956/57 Championship. When he returned Nigel Broomfield blocked his way — for two years — until in 1960 he won the title for the second and last time beating in the final his compatriot T. Shafik. In the following two years — 1961 and 1962 Amin again reached the final but on each occasion was beaten by Michael Oddy. But by now the Australians had arrived. As has happened so often in the past, fitness and speed can curb the best strokes. In 1963 and 1964 Amin was beaten by the new generation of young Australians. But in the Open Championship played before the arrival of the Australians, Amin had one more chance and reached the final. Here, in the only all Egyptian final in this event, Amin was well beaten by Taleb.

Amin was above all a stroke player par excellence. He was also a great sportsman and his perfect demeanour on court won him many admirers. But like all the Egyptians of his generation he did not take kindly to the anti-obstruction rule and paid for this with many penalty points. Always excepting the great Amr, he has more strokes than any other Egyptian, before or since. As secretary of the Egyptian SRA he occasionally visits England as manager of the Egyptian teams.

FATTAH DAVID AMR BEY (AMR PASHA) (1910-   )

It is a fruitless task to compare past with present champions, but those who saw Amr Bey at his best and have watched the present champions are confident that Amr is the greatest. Never has one man so dominated the squash scene as Amr did in the thirties. Hashim? The trouble here is that Hashim was a defensive player who broke his opponents by his incredible speed. But Amr had speed combined with perfect stroke production.

Fattah David Amr Bey, an Egyptian, first visited England as an auxiliary member of the Egyptian Davis Cup lawn tennis team at the age of 18. Shortly after that he returned to England to work in the Egyptian Embassy in London. At that time he was only just starting to play squash. He placed himself in the hands of "Oak" Johnson, the professional at the RAC and turning this pupil into a champion is undoubtedly Johnson's greatest achievement at the game.

Amr won his first Amateur Championship at the age of 21 when he defeated in the final W. D. MacPherson who had already won the Amateur Championship on two occasions. From 1931 to 1938 he was undefeated, winning the Amateur Championship six times (he did not compete in 1934). After his first final, which he only won 9-0 in the fifth game, he did not concede a game and his five finalists could only gather 28 points between them. His record in the Open Championship,

AMR BEY — The Incomparable.

played in those days on a challenge basis, was, if not so devastating, impressive, beating D. G. Butcher twice and J. Dear three times.

Then, as suddenly as he had arrived, he left the squash stage announcing his retirement from Championship play in 1938 when he was still under thirty years of age. For another year he continued to play for the RAC in the Bath Club Cup — and then came the War. In 1935 he had received the unique honour of captaining the British team against the USA in London. Needless to say, playing first string, he won his tie with ridiculous ease.

After the War he returned to London as Egyptian Ambassador — he was still a young man — and was now known as Amr Pasha. After the fall of King Farouk he resigned from the Egyptian Foreign Service and retired to live in Berkshire.

Outside England he played comparatively little. He won the Egyptian Championship while on holiday there in 1936 defeating G. S. Cole a British Army Officer stationed in Egypt 9-4, 9-0, 9-7.

The late Captain V. A. Cazelet, himself a four times winner of the Amateur Championship once wrote: "It is possible as in the case of Amr Bey, to bring the game to such a degree of scientific perfection that a really first class player in a championship may consider himself fortunate if he scores a single point against this remarkable Egyptian".

But apart from his prowess at the game, Amr Pasha will be remembered above all else for his great sportsmanship. Hubert Winterbotham wrote of him: "His old world courtesy, his wonderful spirit of sportsmanship and his unfailing kindliness to young players have introduced a lovable note into a game which, at times, is apt to become a little too grim".

AZAM KHAN (1927-   )

The youngest of the four children of Abadullah Khan, the butler at the Peshawar Club, Azam was for much of his active life overshadowed by his 11 years older brother Hashim. Originally a lawn tennis coach in Pakistan, Azam first came to England with Hashim in the 1953/4 season and immediately made his mark. He reached the final of the Open Championship and played the first of three finals against Hashim. These were not so much championship matches as exhibitions. There is no doubt that Hashim could have won easily, but he chose to make a five game exhibition of each of them. Later when the age gap between the brothers began to tell on the elder, the boot was on the other leg. Azam became professional at the New Grampians Club in London in 1956 and in the following year he became its proprietor in partnership with Hashim. In April 1962 he injured his achilles tendon and though he made a good recovery, never played competitive squash again. His record was second only to that of Hashim. He won both the British Open and the Professional

DON BUTCHER and CHARLES READ — First Open Champions.

Championship of the British Isles four times. His record in America was not so impressive but he won the Canadian Open twice and the US Open once. There are many who think that he could have improved on this had he chosen to. Jonah Barrington played a lot with him and has stated that Azam could beat him at any time even when approaching fifty.

JONAH BARRINGTON (1940-   )

The story of Jonah Barrington is one of the most romantic in the history of squash. His emergence as a champion occurred at a time when the big surge in the game was just beginning and his domination of the game as much as the manner in which he obtained it caught the imagination of the Press and the public. Unlike a number of modern champions such as Broomfield and Oddy, Barrington did not shine at the game as a junior. He certainly played squash at Cheltenham College but without any success. Going on to Trinity College, Dublin, he did manage to get into the College squash team but was more interested in — and good at — downing pints of Guinness than playing squash. He did not last long at Trinity College and then drifted through a number of jobs before a back injury necessitated an operation. It was while recuperating from this that, at the age of 23 he applied for a vacancy at the office of the Squash Rackets Association. His qualifications for the job were meagre and the pay was not very good. Probably because of the latter there was no great rush for the job as assistant secretary, and Jonah got it. The opportunity of playing competitive squash in London worked wonders, and kindled his enthusiasm, starting him on the road to success. In a quite incredibly short space of time he became a first class player and the rest is too well known to need recapitulation. What is of interest in any history of squash rackets is his effect on the game. To the public he was unknown until he became champion. After two unsuccessful appearances in the Amateur Championship his record in other matches entitled him to fifth seeding in the Open Championship in December 1966 which he won, being the first Englishman to win this, the premier event in squash, since 1938. The following month he won the Amateur Championship in which he was seeded fourth, but was taken to five games in both the semi-final and final rounds by the Australians, Hiscoe and Carter. He was the first home player to win the Amateur for five years.

Squash up to that time had not had a good press and of the national dailies, only The Times and the Daily Telegraph regularly published squash results. But Jonah's win tickled the public imagination. Stories of his unique determination, of his ascetic habits (he once called himself the Monk of Kensington), of the unusual jobs he took up after the patience of the Secretary of the SRA had become exhausted, and he had left his job there — all these made him a national character.

JONAH BARRINGTON — Six Times Open Champion.

The name Jonah also helped. There was no need to use his surname in the headlines. There were a number of Barringtons in sport but only one Jonah. He owed much of his early success to the coaching of Nazrullah Khan. A lefthander himself, he did not relish playing other lefthanders, and the Australian Cam Nancarrow in particular who beat him a number of times. Jonah turned professional in 1969. He won the Open Championship of the British Isles six times in all.

He was largely instrumental in forming the International Squash Players Association (ISPA) in 1972 of which he became Chairman.

He is married with two sons.

NORMAN F. BORRETT (1917-   )

Educated at Framlingham and Cambridge University (Pembroke College), Norman Borrett was robbed of his best years by the War. His squash also suffered by reason of his predilection for other games. He represented Cambridge at hockey and also played first class cricket. Although he represented his univerity for three years prior to the War it was not until the 1946 Amateur Championship that he burst upon the national squash scene. Having beaten the top seed Roger Pulbrook in the first round for the loss of seven points, he won the championship with some ease and continued to do so for the following four years before retiring from the game. His duties as a schoolmaster at Framlingham kept him out of competitive squash except in the holidays and he used the early rounds of the Amateur Championship to get much needed practice and play himself into form. Although he dominated squash in the immediate post war years, he played comparatively little after 1951. In 1955 he captained the first British team to play in South Africa. He won only one of his matches in the four Test Matches and did not play competitively again. His game was characterised by severe aggression, hard hitting and speed. His record at hockey was impressive and he captained the British Olympic hockey team in 1948. For many years he represented Devon at cricket. His sporting activities were curtailed by arthritis.

NIGEL H. R. A. BROOMFIELD (1937-   )

Nigel Broomfield was in many respects the perfect amateur. His natural aptitude for all ball games coupled with his fine physique brought him success at squash at a very early age. Educated at Haileybury, he first became junior champion winning the Drysdale Cup at the age of 14, and won this event altogether on three occasions — a record only equalled by Philip Kenyon in 1974. He played for England at the age of 18 and won the first of his two Amateur Championships at 20, being the youngest player at that time to achieve this. He represented Cambridge for three years and toured Australia and South Africa with British teams, winning the South African

NIGEL BROOMFIELD — The Great Amateur.

Championship in 1958. On coming down from Cambridge, he served in the Army, winning the Army Championship on the four occasions for which he entered. Service abroad limited his participation in competitive squash in England and after 1962 he virtually retired. He was the leader of the golden age of British squash, and with J. G. A. Lyon and M. A. Oddy dominated squash in England as well as in other parts of the world. In 1968 he left the Army to join the Foreign Service and has served in this capacity in West Germany and the USSR.

Broomfield was the perfect amateur because he played for enjoyment rather than for gain. He never bothered to train. He was naturally fit and that was enough. He never let squash interfere with his private life. Even if the Service had not taken him out of England so much it is doubtful if he would have continued to play serious squash. He had at an early age achieved the highest ambition of a squash player. Henceforth he would play for exercise and enjoyment.

JAMES PATRICK DEAR, MBE (1910-   )

Jim Dear was born a month after Amr Bey but his competitive life was much longer. Moreover squash was only one of the games at which he excelled. At one time he held the Rackets World Open Championship and the British Professional Championship at Real Tennis. It was his misfortunate to be an exact contemporary of the great Amr, and but for this his solitary victory in the Open Championship would have been repeated several times. Starting as assistant professional at Princes Club at the age of 17, he in 1933 unsuccessfully challenged D. G. Butcher for the Professional Championship of the British Isles, a result which was reversed two years later. Dear had four successive victories in this event in the thirties and came back after the War to win the title once more in 1949.

Three times he unsuccessfully challenged Amr Bey for the Open Championship and in all six matches he put up a fine fight, three of them going to five games. It was after Amr Bey's retirement that in 1938 Dear seized his chance and beat A. E. Biddle of the Junior Carlton to win this title for the only time.

After war service in the RAF (he won the RAF squash championship in 1945) he became rackets and tennis professional at Queens Club.

In 1947 Dear was challenged for the Open title by the Egyptian Mahmoud Kerim. In the last Open Championship to be played on the challenge basis, he was beaten in both matches by the Egyptian and three months later in the first time the championship was played on the knock-out system, Kerim beat Dear again after the English player had had two match balls in the fifth game. Dear continued to play in the Open Championship for a few years but never reached the final

JIM DEAR — The Great All-Rounder.

again. Although he won the Professional Championship of the British Isles in 1950, he gradually gave up squash in favour of rackets at which he remained World Champion until 1954. He worked for some years as professional at Wellington College and (after a brief sojourn in New York) finally settled down at Eton.

HASHIM KHAN (1916-   )

Hashim Khan has many claims to be considered as the greatest player the game has so far seen. He is easily the greatest 'character'. But as a stroke maker he could not hold a candle to either Amr Bey or Mahmoud Karim. He made his reputation on his astonishing speed. He did not come to England until he was 36 but his best years were even then ahead of him. I first saw him playing in the All India Professional Championships when according to his own estimate he was 28, but he did not at that time strike me as being very special.

Hashim was born about the time of the first World War. Mr A. J. Quraishi a well known Pakistan amateur player in the fifties who has undertaken considerable research into the history and genealogy of the Khan family gives the date of Hashim's birth as 1914 whereas Hashim himself in his entertaining book "Squash Rackets" states that he was born in 1916. His father was butler at the Peshawar Club and was killed when Hashim, the oldest of four children, was 11. Hashim spent most of his boyhood in the squash and rackets courts at the Peshawar Club and had the good fortune to be taken under the wing of Abdul Majeed, the club professional who is generally considered to be the grandfather of rackets and squash in India. Majeed's son Ismathullah, who was assistant pro to his father, is credited by Hashim with giving the future champion his first lesson for which Hashim paid four annas.

His first appointment was to the RAF Officers Mess, Peshawar in 1944 and in 1951 Hashim was sent to England to try and emulate the deeds of his cousin Abdul Bari who had come to England the year before. The Pakistan Air Force, fearful lest Hashim's success in England should lure him into taking a job as a professional (as did Abdul Bari), gazetted him a lieutenant in the PAF with good pay and pension rights.

Hashim continued his annual visits to England and in 1953/4 added America to his itinerary. Finally in 1960 he accepted an offer to become professional to a club in Detroit. Hashim was by this time in his middle forties. With the American games less physically demanding he felt that he had a longer active life playing there than trying with increasing difficulty to compete against his younger relatives at the British game. In particular there was his brother Azam. The 1959/60 season was Hashim's last in England. He was beaten by Azam in the semi-final of the Open and had to retire to Jamal Din in the Professional Championship with a hamstring injury. It was the

103

HASHIM KHAN — The Greatest.

writing on the wall and Hashim was astute enough to recognise it as such.

Hashim's record is unsurpassed. Seven times winner of the British Open, and five times of the Professional Championship of the British Isles, his record in America is equally impressive. Three times he won the North American Open and he was also a three time winner of the Canadian Open, the last time in 1964 when he was about 50.

In 1978 Hashim returned to England and won the Open Vintage Championship (for those aged 55 and over). He successfully defended this title in 1979.

KEN J. HISCOE (1938-   )

When the British team visited Australia in 1959 they came up against a young player who had just scraped into the New South Wales team — their first sight of Ken Hiscoe. He played D. B. Hughes and took the first game before Hughes greater experience began to tell. Yet only three years later Hiscoe had improved to the extent that he won the British Amateur Championship, the first Australian to do so. During the sixties he was the leading player in Australia, winning the Australian Amateur Championship six times. On his first visit to England he reached the semi-final of the Amateur Championship having his revenge over Denis Hughes in a five game thriller, and taking I. Amin to five games in the semi-final. In his early days he was a prominent beach life guard. He turned professional with Geoff Hunt in 1971. He became the first President of the International Squash Players Professional Association in 1973. He married in 1970. Hiscoe is above all a stroke player. In addition he is extremely fast and possesses a fine competitive spirit. He has kept his fitness to a remarkable degree and in his fortieth year was still a ranked player. However in 1978 he realised that at his age he could not for much longer continue as a successful circuit player and accepted the post of Australian National Squash Coach.

GEOFFREY BRIAN HUNT (1947-   )

Carefully coached by his father, a Melbourne businessman, Geoff Hunt early became a prodigy and won his first Victorian Championship at the age of 16, having won the Victorian Junior Championship in the previous year. He won the Victorian Championship every year (nine in all) until he turned professional in 1971. He made his first appearance in England in 1964/5 and became at 17 the youngest player to reach the final of the Amateur Championship, but had to wait another five years before winning it. He won the first International Amateur Individual Championship, which was played in his home city in Australia in 1967 and repeated this win in the next two championships in 1969 and 1971. Late in 1971 he unexpectedly turned

GEOFF HUNT — Champion of World Squash in the late seventies.

professional. Until 1971 he was the perfect amateur and did not let his squash interfere with his studies as a result of which he obtained a diploma of applied chemistry at Caulfield Technical College, and became a Bachelor of Science of Monash University. He toured England as an amateur with Jonah Barrington playing a series of matches of which he won a high proportion. But in 1970 and 1972 Barrington defeated Hunt in the final of the Open Championship by slowing down the game and winning a war of attrition. With his natural fitness Geoff Hunt is able to keep at the peak of achievement.

For a while the appearance of the young Pakistani amateurs threatened his dominance in the game, but he won the first World Open Championship which was played in England in 1976, beating the leading Pakistanis in the semi-final and final rounds. He has so far won the British Open Championship six times and the World Championship three times.

He owes his success to his ability to take the ball very early and use controlled aggression for long periods. In 1969 he married Teresa Siciliano, also of Melbourne and has two sons.

MAHMOUD ABDUL KARIM (1914-   )

The son of a Cairo businessman, he was originally a fine lawn tennis and golf player. While at Cairo University Mahmoud played his first game of squash. He finally gave up his University career to become the squash professional at Gezira Club in 1935. Mahmoud — the name by which he was more generally known — first came to this country in the 1946/7 season and promptly challenged J. P. Dear for the Open title. There were several postponements and the first match was not played until December 1947. The Egyptian won easily and won again, much less easily, in the second leg played a few days later. Within three months he successfully defended his title at the first Open Championship to be played as a knock-out tournament. Mahmoud won the Open Championship on four occasions until in 1951 when, unfit he was heavily defeated by the newly arrived Hashim Khan, a defeat which was repeated in the final of the Open the next year. In 1953 Mahmoud made his last appearance in the Open Championship, but an unfortunate collision injured his knee, and although he gave one of his finest exhibitions in winning his match almost on one leg, the injury did not respond to treatment and he was forced to give his next opponent a walkover.

Shortly afterwards Mahmoud emigrated to America and is still at the age of 60 a professional in Montreal. But he never achieved the championship success at the American game which his reputation on this side of the Atlantic led one to expect, probably because the Pakistani Khans crowded him out. Of all the great professionals Mahmoud was — and is — the most graceful mover. He was destroyed by Hashim's speed, but for some years was regarded as the best player in the world.

107

MAHMOUD KARIM — Magic from the Nile.

MOHIBULLAH KHAN, THE ELDER (1938-   )

The son of Hashim's sister who married Rehmatullah's grandson, Safirullah, Mohibullah first came to England in 1957 and reached his first final of the Open Championship in 1959, when he was given a salutary lesson by his uncle, Azam Khan. In his early days Mohibullah is best remembered for his ferocious hitting as well as for his great speed about the court. His early championship performances in England were erratic — in December 1959 he was beaten in the quarter-final by the Scottish amateur M. A. Oddy — but apart from this he reached the final on three occasions, being beaten every time by Azam. It was only after Azam's retirement from competitive play that Mohibullah at last realised his ambition to win the Open. In the final in December 1962 his opponent was the Egyptian A. Taleb. In a memorable match Taleb led the Pakistani by two games to one and 8-1, and held altogether three match balls before Mohibullah won in the fifth game. In the following year he was beaten in the Open semi-final by the same Oddy who had beaten him four years earlier.

In 1963 Mohibullah accepted an appointment in the USA and was not seen again in Europe after the 1963/4 Open. With Hashim past his prime and Azam retired from competitive play, Mohibullah ruled the roost in America, winning the Canadian Open in 1964 immediately before its amalgamation with the US Open, and the latter event four times. His run of successes in this championship was ended by his young cousin Sharif Khan.

MICHAEL ARTHUR ODDY (1937-   )

Michael Oddy was the best squash player ever to come out of Scotland. Together with Nigel Broomfield and Jeremy Lyon he dominated British squash in the late fifties. Oddy, educated at Rugby, lived in Scotland and his appearances as a junior in London were less than those of the other two. Although the same age as Broomfield, he did not compete in the Drysdale Cup until a year after Broomfield had won it, and he had to wait until 1956 when Broomfield and Lyon had finished with this tournament before winning it at the age of 18. But a few months before this he had become the youngest ever winner of the Scottish Amateur Championship, an event he won five times in all. He first played in the Amateur Championship in 1957 when by a gross piece of mismanagement by the Championship Committee, he was opposed in the first round by Scotland's leading player, Ian de Sales la Terriere. He had to wait until 1961 before becoming Amateur Champion, beating in the final both that year and the following the Egyptian I. Amin. In 1963 he became the first amateur since 1952 to reach the final of the Open Championship by virtue of an unexpected win in the semi-final over Mohibullah Khan, but was soundly beaten by Taleb. He won the Australian Amateur Championship in 1959 and the South African Championship in 1962. Illness and the claims of business compelled him to give up serious competitive play although he made a fleeting reappearance for Rugby in the Londonderry Cup in the early seventies. In the mid-seventies he left Scotland and settled in Leicester, where he still plays in the Inter-County Championship and in the Midlands League.

JAMES EDWARD PALMER-TOMKINSON (1879-1961)

The first great English player to emerge once the game became competitive, Captain 'Jimmy' Palmer-Tomkinson was 43 years old when the first Amateur Championship was played in 1922. Defeated in the final of that event by T. O. Jameson, Palmer-Tomkinson was also runner-up in 1924 and 1925 before at the age of 47 he won the event in 1926 in which he defeated Victor Cazelet (who had beaten him in the final the previous year). In 1905 he first won the handicap competition at the Bath Club, and for the next twenty years was the leading amateur in England.

On the formation of the Squash Rackets Association in 1929 he became the first Chairman of the Executive Committee, a post which he held until, in 1947, he became President, from which he retired only a few months before his death at the age of 81. His work as an administrator was little known or appreciated, but his sage advice in the early days of squash as a popular game had much to do with the successful growth of the game at that time and in particular he worked untiringly, although in his late sixties, to rebuild the SRA after the War.

ROSHAN KHAN (1927-   )

The two great squash families in Pakistan, descendants of Rehmatullah and Muhammad Ali were joined when Rehmatullah's granddaughter married Faizullah Khan, the grandson of Muhammad Ali. Roshan Khan was the second son of this marriage and was seven years younger than Nazrullah Khan, who coached in England for 20 years. He first played in England in 1954 and made an immediate impact beating in his first tournament in the semi-final, Azam, and in the final, Mahmoud Kerim. Hashim beat him in five games in the semi-final of the Professional Championship while in the semi-final of the Open, Azam had his revenge over Roshan in five games.

Roshan only won the Open Championship once (in 1957 when he beat Hashim, who was suffering from a leg injury). He won the US Open three times. Of the great triumvirate of Pakistani players — Hashim, Azam and Roshan, the last named was undoubtedly the best stroke player. He was feared by Hashim who saw him as a serious threat to Hashim's plan for Azam to take over as the world's leading player when the time should come for Hashim to stand down. While

Hashim and Azam had been identified with the Pakistan Air Force, Roshan was employed by the Pakistan Navy. He has not been to England for a number of years, but his son Torsam Khan is practising as a professional in England.

ABOU TALEB (1939-   )

Taleb first came to England for the 1961/2 season, already with a considerable reputation in his native Egypt where he had beaten the redoubtable Dardir. He was stockily built and it was not long before he began to have weight problems. His wide repertoire of strokes mesmerised his opponents, and his carefree approach to the game went down well as long as he was winning. Towards the end of his reign he indulged in certain practices in court which made him less popular. In his first Open Championship in December 1961 he was given a salutary lesson in the quarter-finals by Mohibullah Khan, but next year he did everything but win against the same player, having three match balls in the fourth game of the final. In December 1963 his task was made easier by Michael Oddy who defeated Mohibullah in the semi-final. Taleb won the first of his three Championships with some ease. In the following year he beat fellow compatriot I. Amin in the final, and in 1964 he won his last Championship when he beat the Pakistani, A. Jawaid in four games. Then, in December 1966 came Taleb's famous match with Jonah Barrington in the quarter-finals. Taleb lost because everything he did on that day, Jonah did better. It was sad to see a reigning champion go down but Taleb lost much sympathy by his rough tactics on court. The next year Taleb reached the final of the Open, but was taken to five games by amateurs in each of the preceeding two rounds. He was unable to put up much opposition to Barrington in the final, once the first game had gone against him. By the time the next Open Championship was played — in February 1969 — the Australians had arrived and increasing weight weakened any chance Taleb might have had in regaining the title.

In Egypt he had been professional at the Heliopolis Club in Cairo and he continued to dominate the Egyptian Championship until in 1969 he settled down as a professional in England.

CHAPTER VIII

THE PROFESSIONAL
AND AMATEUR GAMES

THE PROFESSIONALS

*T*HE EARLY professionals all started as rackets professionals or, in a few cases, as real tennis pros. Most of them taught at the public schools, and the rest either at Queens or Princes Clubs. Later on, a number of lawn tennis pros added squash to their curricula although they had no qualifications either as players or teachers. With a number of lawn tennis clubs adding squash courts, it gave the pro an extra string to his bow to have the opportunity of earning some money in the English winter when opportunities of coaching tennis were limited.

When the London West End Social Clubs built squash courts, it was considered necessary for the larger clubs to have a pro on hand not only to give instruction, but mainly to be able to give the members a game whenever required. By 1938 there were 110 squash professionals in the UK made up as follows:

Attached to Clubs (excluding London West End Clubs)	59
London West End Social Clubs	23
Schools	16
Freelance	12
	——
	110

It is interesting to compare these figures with 1976, the latest year for which figures are available. The breakdown in that year was:

Attached to Clubs (excluding London West End Clubs)   40

London West End Clubs	2
Schools	3
Freelance	55
Playing Professionals	3
Overseas	3
Women	12
	118

It should be borne in mind that the 1976 figures refer only to members of the Squash Rackets Professionals Association. It is probable that a number of schools rackets pros have not bothered to join this body. It is sad to note the greatly reduced numbers of professionals at the London West End Clubs. The numbers of such clubs having their own courts has fallen in the same period from 27 to 10. The impressive rise of freelance pros from 12 to 55 also needs some explanation. This figure undoubtedly includes many coaches who took advantage of the Approved Amateur Coaches scheme to reap some reward from their part time coaching. While this is strictly controlled and limited by the SRA a number of these grey area amateurs began to make so much money that they were informed by the SRA that they could not continue in this way without sacrificing their amateur status, which some of them accordingly did. Then there are a number of professionals who are not employed by a single club but spread their services over a number of clubs.

But perhaps the greatest surprise is that the number of professionals has not risen. To understand this better it is worth while to consider an intermediate year — say 1960, when the position was:

Attached to Clubs (excluding London West End Clubs)	26
London West End Clubs	10
Schools	6
Freelance	20
Overseas	13
	75

This was just before the commencement of the squash boom, but the economic situation had clearly caused a certain number of casualties among the West End Social Clubs. Also in those days women were not eligible to join the professional body.

Going back to the early days, the professionals provided the best players, because in those days squash was very much of a secondary pursuit among the gentry. It was natural that members of the West End Clubs should consider that their own pro was superior to any others and this resulted in a number of challenge matches for purses put up by the members. In 1920 one such of these was designated the Professional Championship of the British Isles, as a result of which Charles Read of Queens beat Oak Johnson (RAC) on aggregate winning 3-0 at Queens and losing 1-3 at the RAC. Nothing more happened under this heading until 1925 when there was a repeat performance between the same two players with much the same result.

On the strength of this, when the Open Championship was instituted in 1930, Charles Read was designated as Champion which was perhaps unfortunate, for Read, then 41 years old, was past his best and was in the same year decisively beaten by Donald Butcher of the Conservative Club for the Professional Championship. The position was regularised in the following year when Butcher beat Read in challenge matches for the Open Championship, winning 9-6, 9-5, 9-5 at Queens and 9-3, 9-5, 9-3, at the Conservative.

Read was born in 1889, a year before Johnson, but the oldest of the three most famous pros at that time was Charles Arnold, pro at the Bath Club and born in 1884. It was Arnold who taught the Prince of Wales (later King Edward VIII) to play, and used the three feathers with the Royal Warant, the only time the Warrant has been awarded for squash. Arnold blossomed as a player fairly late in life and challenged Butcher for the Open title in 1931 getting a fearful hammering at the Conservative Club in which he failed to score a point, and collecting only eight points at the Bath Club.

The three, Read, Johnson and Arnold, all great friends were popularly known as the Three Musketeers, and were the leaders of their craft for many years. Read was the greatest of them for in addition to his skill at squash he was professional lawn tennis champion (1921/8) and professional rackets champion (1925/31). He died in 1962 having retired to live in Sussex some years before. But he was game to the end and played in the Professional Championship in 1954 at the age of 65, when W. J. Ashford beat him 9-3, 9-4, 9-0.

Oak Johnson came to squash by accident. He was engaged by the RAC as a real tennis pro, but at the last moment the projected tennis court in the Pall Mall premises of the club was changed into a swimming pool and squash courts so that Johnson took over the squash. His most famous pupil was Amr Bey who acknowledged that he owed much of his success to Johnson's coaching. He continued at the RAC long after he was able to play the game seriously, and one of his last pupils was Nigel Broomfield, when that precocious player first won the Drysdale Cup in 1952 at the age of 15. Johnson continued to coach from the gallery and was active in this way right up to the time of his death in 1965.

Charles Arnold after 25 years as pro at the Bath Club transferred to the Kensington Country Club in 1937 but gradually went into the squash court construction business, and after the War was with Grays of Cambridge for many years. He died in 1974, aged 90.

In the early days there were few professionals outside England but it was known that there were a number attached to British Army Garrison stations in India. Returning soldiers told of the prowess of some of them. During the War, I was stationed for a time in Bombay and got to know Abdul Bari, the pro at the Cricket Club of India. In

1944 it was decided to play the West of India Amateur Championship and the All-India Professional Championship on the CCI courts in that city, and I was invited to assist in running the latter event. We were all expecting an easy win for Abdul Bari but in the final he came up against a comparatively unknown player from the Punjab who beat Bari handsomely. This was none other than Hashim Khan.

I was tremendously impressed by the courteous demeanour and charm, as well as the technical skill of Abdul Bari. While in Bombay I expressed to the squash authorities there my hope that after the War it might be possible for a team of Indian professionals to visit England. This hope was partly realised in 1950 when the members of the CCI put up the funds to send Bari to England to play in the Open Championship. While he was here I learned that he was not too happy in Bombay and when in 1952 Bert Biddle, pro at the Junior Carlton Club was compelled to resign on grounds of ill health, I, as captain of squash at that club offered the post to Bari. He arrived early in 1953, the first professional from the Indian sub-continent to become a pro in England. It was a bold experiment, but Bari won all hearts by his charm as well as by the excellence of his squash, both as player and teacher. It was tragic that after only 21 months he died of a brain tumour. To replace him I engaged another professional this time from Pakistan. This was even more of a gamble for I had never to my knowledge met him. But my luck held for this was Nazrullah Khan, probably the greatest teaching professional to come out of the East.

In the meantime Hashim Khan had begun his series of wins in the Open Championship and in 1953 he brought with him his younger brother Azam, and in 1956 Azam was installed as manager and professional at the New Grampians Squash Club in London, which his elder brother had helped him to buy.

But to return to the thirties. After the Three Musketeers, Don Butcher took over as the acknowledged best professional. His reign was comparatively brief for after two wins in the Open Championship he fell to the brilliance of Amr Bey who beat him twice. Butcher won the Professional Championship of the British Isles (which at that time was also played on a challenge basis) on three occasions beating Read (1930), Arnold (1931) and J. P. Dear (1933), but Dear beat Butcher in 1935 and 1936. Butcher left the Conservative Club in 1936 to join the St Johns Wood SRC, which in addition to three singles courts had a doubles court. After the War, Butcher was at the Lansdowne Club for a short time before going to the Hampstead S & RFC, where he remained until in 1955 he emigrated to Australia, where he died in 1976.

Jim Dear, like Charles Read before him, was a great all-rounder. His name will always be associated with Princes Club and it was while there that he won the Open Championship in 1939 having on three previous challenges been thwarted by Amr Bey. Amr used to practice for the defence of his title with A. E. Biddle of the Junior Carlton, and this was the player whom Dear defeated in 1939. As Amr was an amateur, Dear's pre-eminence as a professional lasted longer in the Professional Championship of the British Isles, which he won on four occasions. During the War he served in the RAF, picking up that Championship in 1946. Returning to resume his squash career, he joined Queens Club and won the Professional Championship (whch after the War had become a tournament) in 1950 beating Abdul Bari. He was the greatest all-rounder of his generation at racket games holding the World Rackets title from 1947-54 and World Real Tennis title from 1955-57. These activities somewhat curtailed his squash career and after the 1950/51 season he retired from competitive squash — by this time he was 42! — to concentrate on the less exhausting games of rackets and real tennis. His natural successor among British professionals was Bert Biddle, professional at the Junior Carlton Club from 1929 until his retirement through ill health in 1953. Biddle, like many others, was robbed of his best competitive years by the War. After unsuccessfully challenging Dear for the Open Championship in 1939, and for the Professional Championship in 1938 and 1939, he lost in the final of the latter to Leslie Keeble in 1948, but had his revenge in the same final in the following year. He was only 45 when he died.

J. H. Giles started his professional career at Charterhouse School before the War, and after that moved to Abbeydale (Sheffield). The retirement of Oak Johnson gave him the chance to return to London and he has been pro at the RAC since 1956. After the War and with the retirement from squash of Jim Dear, Jack Giles was rightly regarded as the best of the home professionals. But with more and more overseas pros coming to this country from Pakistan and Egypt he had little chance of making much money out of competitions. By the early fifties the only annual tournaments for the home pros were the Open and Professional Championships of the British Isles.

After the War, Grays of Cambridge and the Silvertown ballmaking company held professional tournaments, but these events were not followed up. Dunlops started a tournament in 1948 which was played in alternate years on six occasions. In the first year Dear reached the final, but otherwise the later rounds were invariably fought out by overseas players, who made money in other parts of the world and, latterly, were used by Hashim and Azam to give an exhibition of their skills, which was not the object of the exercise, so this too was dropped.

Finally, Mr J. P. Mitchelhill, a member of the RAC, presented a cup for a competition to be called the Professional Championship of the United Kingdom, open only to professionals born and practising in the United Kingdom. This was first played at the Hampstead S & RFC in November 1954 and attracted an entry of 20. This was one more than that received for the previous seasons Professional Championship of the British Isles when all four seeds were overseas players. Jack Giles won this new event. But the bright start did not last and after three years as a tournament the rules were changed, turning the event from a knock-out tournament to the challenge system. Whether it was that the professionals could not afford the time lost from coaching, or the expenses of competing, or whether the low standard of play of the average English professional made him wary of competing against the better players, the fact remained that it had become increasingly difficult to obtain a sufficient number of entries to make worthwhile the holding of a professional knock-out tournament. Moreover, the apathy of the public made the gate money insufficient to provide just rewards for the successful competitors. In other words the public preferred to spend their money watching the Pakistanis. The new format worked tolerably well for with the Championship decided by matches at the home clubs of holder and challenger, there were always sufficient spectators who would pay to see their own pro in action. By modern standards the returns were pitifully meagre. This was, of course, before the days of sponsorship. The change of format did not make any difference as far as the winner was concerned and Jack Giles continued to win until with ten wins to his credit he chose to quit. Even so, on four occasions there were no challengers.

The poor remuneration received by squash professionals in this country inevitably led a number of the more adventuresome seeking their fortune overseas. Of these the most notable were Bill Aylott (Canada), Tony Barnes (South Africa), Derek Bocquet (Canada), Bill Clements (Rhodesia), Bob Giles, brother of Jack (USA), Don McLaggan (USA), Jim McQueenie (Canada) and Jack Vere (Rhodesia). Even the great Jim Dear capitulated, lured by the good money to be earned in the USA and went as tennis pro to the Tennis and Racquet Club in New York. But after a few years he returned to England and is now at Eton.

The professionals formed their own association in the early thirties with Arnold as their Chairman. However a dispute with the SRA over the ball to be used for the Amateur Championship not only led to Arnold leaving the Bath Club, where the Championships were played, but also the dissolution of the professionals association. After that the pros became professional members of the SRA with their own committee, the chairman and vice-chairman of which were amateurs. Jack Giles was secretary of the professionals committee from 1965-75 and when he was succeeded by Major A. E. Millman it was decided that the professionals who were rapidly increasing in number, should have their own association once more. The Squash Rackets Professional Association is an energetic body and Ted Millman runs a number of events including an annual championship for its members. By the middle of 1976 the breakdown of the membership was:

British professionals practising in England   93
British professionals practising abroad   3

Foreigners practising in England	17
Women	12
	——
	125

The members of this organisation are predominantly teaching professionals although the leading British playing professionals such as Jonah Barrington, J. N. C. Easter and B. Patterson are also members. But if a five a side match between British and foreign members were to be played, the odds would be on the latter winning.

The formation of the professional circus and the marked increase in the number of tournaments open to professionals, plus some disputes between the tournament organisers and the professionals, led to the formation in 1974 of ISPPA, the International Squash Players Professional Association (at a later date the 'Professional' was dropped from the title). This is an association of professional players who were involved in Open tournament play throughout the world. Ken Hiscoe was elected President, Jonah Barrington, Chairman, and Geoff Hunt, Vice-President. The aims were stated to be to provide the professional player with a higher standard of living and playing and to protect that body's interests on an international basis; to liaise and work with all the governing bodies, tournament organisations, and the sponsors, and to safeguard the future development of competitive professionals throughout the world.

There can be no doubt that there is ample need for such an organisation, the main weakness of which is that the committee members are seldom in any one country at the same time. It is a great advantage for sponsors to have an organised body to deal with in discussing details of their sponsorship, which consists largely of money prizes going to members of ISPA. In the early days of its existence ISPA tried to exercise too much power as when they interferred with the prizes given to amateurs in an Open tournament. But in general ISPA has justified itself and is invaluable when professionals have to be seeded in tournament draws. ISPA from time to time issues ranking lists of its chief members. They have taken over the organising of the World Open championship and have laid down at what time of year their members will be available to play in certain countries.

WOMEN AND SQUASH

There can be no doubt that women's squash started in the private courts of country houses. Brothers introduced the game to their sisters and fathers to daughters. The growth of womens squash was accordingly slow. The London West End clubs, which did so much to popularise the game in the third and fourth decades of this century, were not open to women and the first female club to build squash courts was the Ladies Carlton Club in Grosvenor Place, a club which also had the foresight to build the only doubles court in London's West End, destroyed, alas, in the War.

But women's squash had already obtained a foothold in the game and changing facilities for women were included in most of the squash clubs constructed in England in the twenties and thirties. Before this, however, women played the game at Queens, the mixed sporting club in West London. E. B. Noel was secretary of the club for many years and his daughter Susan, with facilities of playing and coaching so easily at hand, became the leading player in the early thirties in which she won the Womens Championship three times in addition to winning the Ladies Championship of the USA. Squash Rackets is unique in that the Womens Championship was started in the same year as the mens — 1922, in which year there were in fact two championships, the first in the spring of that year, and the second in the following December. The venue, of course, was Queens — nowhere else were there changing facilities! It was Queens who presented the Challenge Cup for the winner.

The early championships were dominated by the Cave sisters, Joyce and Nancy, and in the first ten championships they figured as winner or runner-up on no less than 14 occasions, with each sister winning three times. Nancy was the older of the two. Both sisters were noted for their strong wrists and their ability to take back-hand shots from behind them with an easy flick of the wrist. Joyce was slightly the speedier of the two and was reckoned to be just the better player.

After the Cave sisters came Cecily Fenwick who won three Championships in addition to being runner up twice. Her wrist was not as strong as those of the Cave sisters but her placings were better.

The early thirties saw Susan Noel's three championships, and when she retired rather early, she was succeeded by Margot Lumb, a wonderful lefthander who was almost as good at lawn tennis and played in the Wightman Cup. Her father trained and looked after her very much as did the father of Suzanne Lenglen. Margot was not allowed to mix with other women squash players and after a match was hustled away by her father. No parties or gaiety for Margot! When going to America to compete in the Wolfe-Noel Cup matches she and her father travelled first class while the other members of the team went tourist in the same ship!

Perhaps the best player never to win the Championship in those pre-war days was the Hon Anne Lytton-Milbanke, later Lady Anne Lytton and President of the WSRA from 1948 until her retirement in 1975. She died in 1979. She was a wonderful retriever and reached the final twice, only to be beaten by Margot Lumb. Her best years were much earlier in the twenties when she usually reached the semi-finals, but was then beaten by Cecily Fenwick. Margot Lumb won five championships in a row, a record at that time, but then came the War and marriage to Major W. H. L. Gordan, who himself played for the Army after the War. Margot followed her husband to Uganda and was lost to all competitive activities thereafter.

After the War another player who was well known as a tennis player, Joan Curry from Devon, won the first three championships. She is chiefly remembered as a retriever and in her last two championships she beat in the final Janet Morgan, who in February 1950 started on a reign of 10 years before back trouble forced her to retire, and the championship went to Sheila Macintosh, nee Speight, who had been runner up to Janet on five occasions. In 1966 Heather Blundell arrived from Australia and began her remarkable series of wins which continued until 1978 when she decided not to compete. Heather, who had married Brian McKay, another Australian in 1965 now, with her husband runs a squash club in Toronto.

But to return to Janet Morgan, who in addition to her squash was a top class lawn tennis player who competed at Wimbledon for 12 years. She is undoubtedly the best player England has produced and during her reign as Womens champion there was no player to equal her. She set up a record which not even Heather McKay has beaten by winning the Womens championships of England, the USA and Australia in the same season (1954/5). She did not start playing the game until she was 25 and won her first English title three years later. One of the secrets of her success is that she was the first woman player to have done serious 'off court' training for the game. She was undoubtedly helped in this by her profession of a PE teacher. She played an almost masculine game hitting the ball harder than any woman of her time. She gave a great deal back to the game and has worked tirelessly for squash both before and since her retirement from the game, and her services were very rightly rewarded by the award of the MBE in 1971.

Although the first Womens Championship was played in 1922 it was another twelve years before the Womens SRA was formed with Nancy Cave as the first Chairman. There were 15 affiliated clubs and 63 members. At the time of its formation there were only four competitions for women apart from the Womens Championship, of which the senior were the South of England Championship and the Womens London Inter-Club Cup; both started in 1931. One of the hinderences to the growth of the women's game was that for many years it was not played in schools. It was not until 1950 that the Girls Junior championship was started. This now regularly receives an entry of 64 at least, although there was a period of six years from 1962 to 1967 when there was no competition. No winner of the Junior Championship has gone on to win the senior event but Anna Craven-Smith, who won the junior title in 1960, was three times runner-up to Heather McKay in the Womens Championship.

In 1933 a British team sailed to America to see if their players could overcome the difficulties of playing under the different conditions of the American game. A cup was presented jointly by Mrs G. Bryans-Wolfe, the non-playing captain of the British team, and Susan Noel at that time Womens Champion, to be played for annually if possible, by teams representing Great Britain and the USA. Thus was born the Wolfe-Noel Cup, the only regular competitive event between the British and American games. The first match, played at the Sleepy Hollow Club near New York was won by the British team 4-1. Susan Noel also won the American Womens National Championship as well as the Atlantic Coast Championship, while her team mate, Cecily Fenwick won the New York State Championship defeating Susan in the final.

The next three contests played in the USA were all won by the home team, but after the War Great Britain won twice in the USA. In London, Great Britain never lost even a tie, thus again proving that it is more difficult to change from the American game to the British than vice versa.

Sadly, the economics of the game have made it impossible for Great Britain to send a team to the States for nearly 10 years, but there have been signs that the women's competitive game in the States is not as sharp as it was 20 years ago. This is possibly accounted for by the tremendous growth of lawn tennis; played indoors at all times of the year, it may well have robbed squash of many American women with a good eye for games who might otherwise have devoted their energy to squash.

As competition for the Wolfe-Noel Cup declined, British womens squash players faced challenges from other overseas countries, and the task of sending British teams to Australia and South Africa absorbed not only the energies but also the cash of the WSRA and the players. British women toured South Africa in 1963 and won the Test Series 3-0, but were themselves beaten by a similar score when they toured Australia two years later. In the five series so far played between Great Britain and Australia, in both countries, the Australians have always won. They had the enormous advantage of being led by Heather McKay, but even apart from her, the Australian women have shown themselves superior to the British women in recent years. Against South Africa, while Great Britain won the first series easily in 1963 and again in 1968, the South African girls improved and reversed the result in 1973 in South Africa, while New Zealand also beat Great Britain in 1972 and 1973.

The British team went to Australia in 1976 to compete in the first Women's World Championship, and the opportunity was taken to play a Test Match in Sydney before the Championship. Australia, for whom Heather McKay, now a professional was not eligible, again won 2-1 but Britain's Sue Cogswell had the satisfaction of winning the top string against Sue Newman.

In the Championship, however, British girls performed poorly and were eliminated by the end of the third round. Australia's Sue Newman won the event easily beating in the final South Africa's Jill Eckstein.

As already stated Heather McKay turned professional in 1974, and in the same year emigrated with her husband Bryan to Canada. Heather is one of the most remarkable sporting types to come out of Australia, that paradise of sport. There can be few players of any individual sport who can play undefeated for 15 years. It was in January 1962 that Fran Marshall beat the 20 year old Australian, making her first tour in England. Within a month, in the final of the Womens Championship, Heather had reversed the result beating Fran Marshall 3-0 in half an hour to become the youngest competitor to win this event, and to start her long reign. Before emigrating to Canada, Heather ran a squash complex in Sydney and played almost all her squash against men, since only men could provide her with adequate opposition. Indeed she plays a mans game and could comfortably beat some men who play in the Amateur Championship. Yet Hashim Khan, aged 60 +, recently beat her at the American game. Her services to squash were fittingly recognised by the award of the MBE.

Squash is one of the severest challenges in sport to the human body. It is for this reason that women have never been able to play men on an equal footing. For many years teams representative of the top players of both sexes have played in an annual match between the WSRA and the SRA. The women receive one hand, three points and they alone have the benefit of American scoring, winning a stroke whether they are in hand or not. Daunting odds by any standard, yet the men almost invariably win, although the matches are desperately close.

There are many reasons why men and women cannot compete on an equal footing. For one thing women cannot by the nature of their build turn as quickly as can men, and their backs are also weaker. A few women have an almost masculine frame and these have an advantage over other women at squash. Finally womens feet are smaller than mens making balance more difficult.

JUNIOR SQUASH

The growth of squash at schools was in the early days restricted by the senior game of rackets. Any youngster who showed promise at rackets was often barred from playing squash by the rackets pro — Colin Cowdrey was one such — the theory being that squash was bad for rackets. In addition, squash was looked down upon by headmasters and it has only recently been recognised as a school game at many schools. In this it followed closely the history of lawn tennis. Moreover squash was not considered a 'team game' and was not supposed to inculcate team spirit in the same way as cricket or rugger.

But rackets has always been an expensive game to play and as time went on more and more parents were happier with their sons playing squash on purely economic grounds. Moreover one of the chief drawbacks of rackets is the shortage of courts outside the public schools, and the difficulty of continuing to play once a boy has left school. Here squash scored heavily. There are, in fact, only about a dozen schools which now possess rackets courts, and all these have squash courts in addition. Gradually the advantages of squash over rackets had to be faced and while the old rackets pros are still to some extent naturally prejudiced in favour of the game for which they were appointed, the number of boys playing the cheaper game has far outstripped the rackets players at the public schools.

The expansion of squash at schools has been steady and has to a great extent followed the expansion of the game. There were few schools with courts before the 1914/18 War, and not many were built for some years after the 1939/45 War. There are now nearly 120 schools possessing their own courts, which total over 250. The most significant change in recent years has been in the types of schools building courts. It is safe to say that every public school has courts but nowadays Grammar and Comprehensive schools are building courts. Also about a dozen Preparatory Schools have courts. Statistics are difficult to compile because a number of schools do not bother to affiliate their courts to their County association.

Overseas, very few schools are lucky enough to have their own squash courts and this has been a big deterrent to the development in junior squash in other countries. An exception to this is South Africa where Diocesans College (Cape Town) and Michaelhouse (Natal) two of the principal schools have courts at the schools. In Australia many schools have block bookings at public courts, but neither here nor in other countries is there anything like the amount of junior competitive squash that is to be found in the United Kingdom.

JUNIOR COMPETITIONS

Junior competitions were slow to make their appearance. The first was the Evans Cup started at Queens Club as long ago as 1922. There were, in fact, only three other junior tournaments started before the 1939 War — the Drysdale Cup (1926), the Devon Junior Championship (1934) and the South of England Junior Championship (1939).

The most famous of these is the Drysdale Cup which for many years was recognised as the unofficial junior championship. This was organised by the RAC (it is now run by the SRA) and the cup given in memory of Dr T. Drysdale, one of the club's most prominent sporting members. The competition was first played in April 1926, but what is not so well known is that it was Dr Drysdale himself who first suggested the tournament to a meeting of the Representatives Committee in March 1925, and offered to present a challenge cup. At a subsequent meeting it was left to Dr Drysdale to form the inevitable sub-committee to lay down the conditions and to make the arrangements for what was at first simply called the Junior Amateur Squash Championship. Unfortunately Dr Drysdale died before the tournament started and the RAC took over the arrangements.

Members of the club subscribed to the cost of the Cup, which was presented in memory of the doctor. The first tournament was held in April 1926. There were 30 entries and the best of three games was played — scoring at that time was still the same as in rackets, i.e. 15 up.

In 1927 the Tennis and Rackets Association decided to leave this tournament entirely in the hands of the RAC, and it was run by the squash committee of that club until taken over by the SRA in 1978. It has never sought, nor been accorded official recognition by the SRA as the Junior Championship although it was always so regarded the world over. So much so that young players from overseas started to come to England in order to compete. First of the invaders was Peter Gerlow from Denmark who competed for the first time in 1960 when he was just 17 and already Danish National Champion. In this year he reached the semi-final but went on to win the tournament in the succeeding two years. In 1963 Sharif Khan, son of Hashim and at school in England won the tournament having made his first appearance in the competition three years earlier.

In 1965 Anil Nayar came to England with the prestige of being Indian National Champion. In spite of this he was unseeded but only P. R. Goodwin, who took him to five games in the semi-final, gave the talented young Indian any trouble. This year also saw the beginning of the Dutch challenge with Willem Van Rooyen. For a number of years there was always at least one Dutchman in the draw, but although they sometimes reached the final so far none has succeeded in capturing the title. In 1971 a team of five young Swedes appeared for the first time. In that year also there made the one and only appearance of a fourteen year old boy sent over by the Pakistan SRA and called simply Mohibullah. Dropping only 15 points in five rounds he proved the easiest winner in the history of the Cup. The next year his entry was not received until after the draw had taken place and the RAC quite rightly declined to make a new draw.

While a number of players have won the Drysdale Cup twice, only one player — Nigel Broomfield — has won it three times. It should have been four times but in 1953 Broomfield exhausted himself playing friendly matches against well known adult players on the day before the final. Against Jeremy Lyon in the final he won the first game and obtained a lead in the second before exhaustion set in.

It is perhaps surprising that so far only two winners of the Drysdale Cup, Broomfield and M. A. Oddy, have gone on to win the Amateur Championship, although many have achieved international honours.

As has been already stated, the Evans Cup was started three years before the Drysdale. The latter was for players under 19 about three months prior to the start of the competition, but the Evans was for those under 18. The Drysdale is played in the Easter vacation, the Evans was always held in early January. Played originally at Queens Club, the destruction in the War of the squash courts there made a change necessary. After various venues had been tried it settled down at the Junior Carlton Club but was discontinued in 1968 when that Club was pulled down. Originally the competition was played on a handicap basis but from 1950 onwards was played level. Played in conjunction with the Evans Cup was the "Public Schools (under 16) Tournament", commonly called the Junior Evans Cup. That infant prodigy Broomfield won both the Evans and the Junior Evans twice in the same year (he won the Evans Cup four time all told). In 1967 the Junior Evans moved to the RAC and is still played there in the Christmas vacation.

The vast increase in sponsorship has spread to junior tournaments and recently Falcoln Inns Ltd, have sponsored a British Junior Championships with Under-19 and Under-16 events, while the same company now sponsors nine Area Junior Championships. There is also a sponsored Under-14 Championship.

Inter school team contests were for some years frowned upon by the headmasters but in 1968 the Bath Club started a tournament in the Christmas vacation for three-a-side teams which has become popular. It is not restricted to public schools and was won for three years running by Huddersfield New College. In 1972 Premier Products Ltd, started a national inter schools contest which attracted 90 schools in its first year and which was played throughout the season with the finals played at Wembley in March.

Before the start of the Under-14 Championship, the younger players were catered for by the Surrey Championships Under-15 event, but in 1969 Mr Brian Belle, a well-known Preparatory Schools headmaster, formed a squash committee of the Incorporated Association of Preparatory Schools and the result has been a tournament for singles and doubles Prep school boys which has grown from strength to strength.

Of the many county junior championships, one of the oldest and certainly the largest is the Surrey Junior Championship, which has a senior and a junior event as well as Schools Doubles (in 1974 an Under-21 event was added). The Preparatory Schools Doubles Cup was handed over to Mr Belle's new competition in 1969.

In 1938 the Lonsdale Cup was inaugurated for Public Schools Open Doubles Competition. It was played at the St Johns Wood doubles court. After the War it was renewed at the Bath Club and played concurrently with the Drysdale Cup, but was discontinued after 1970.

While the competitors in junior tournaments were in the early days almost exclusively from the public schools, this monopoly no longer exists. Many grammar and technical schools have taken up squash even though they may not possess courts of their own. For three years the Bath Club Inter-Schools Tournament was won by Huddersfield New College which does not possess courts. Twenty-eight counties now have junior championships, many with more than one age group.

Finally, the barrier between squash and rackets seems to be

breaking down and history was made in 1976 when the finalists of the Middlesex Under-16 Championships were the same players who had fought out only the day before the final of the Public Schools Under-16 Rackets Championship.

JUNIOR INTERNATIONAL SQUASH

Tony Swift, senior British National Coach from 1972/76 had the foresight to realise that the future of a country at squash depends on catching them young — and providing international competition at an early age. Prior to Tony becoming junior supremo there had been little interchange of national junior teams. An Egyptian junior team had visited England in 1968 and a team from Michaelhouse School, South Africa also made a tour of England in 1974, but these were isolated instances and there were no regular visits until Sweden started sending players to take part in junior tournaments in England in 1971. Lack of competition play prevented the young Swedes from making much impression on the English juniors, but the opportunity was taken to play a match against an English junior team.

In 1973 Tony Swift thought up the idea of a junior international festival to coincide with the Drysdale Cup, when the top juniors would be in London. With great help from the National Westminster Bank, who donated a trophy and made their courts available, the First Junior International Festival was held at Sydenham in April 1973 with teams representing England, Wales, Scotland and Sweden. As was to be expected England won easily but the Swedish boys played well and beat the juniors of Wales and Scotland. In the following year Sweden dropped out but their place was taken by the visiting Michaelhouse South African team. In 1975 the venue was Edinburgh and with Sweden again absent, an Egyptian team made up the number. In 1976 Sweden returned to the competition to take Egypt's place. The Swedes easily beat Ireland, Wales and Scotland but could not win a tie from England although three of the matches went to five games.

In 1975 a British junior team, managed by Tony Swift toured South Africa and won all their matches including three Test Matches.

SERVICE SQUASH

The fighting forces of the world do not spend all their time fighting, thank goodness, and what to do with them when they are merely engaged in garrison duty has always been a problem. Maintenance of fitness has always figured high on the list of priorities and to this end the provision of sports facilities has always figured largely, sport being more attractive than endless PT. It must be admitted that the Officers, at any rate of the ground forces, had more leisure time than the other ranks and it therefore came about that particularly in the North West of India, where there were always in the late nineteenth century large numbers of troops guarding the Khyber Pass, the various Officers Clubs provided sports facilities including in the early days even rackets courts. The dawning popularity of squash in the closing days of the last century prompted many of these clubs to transform the rackets courts into squash courts as a result of which more officers could get their exercise in a shorter time, and much cheaper. Thus it came about that a number of ball boys — for by this time lawn tennis was rapidly gaining popularity — took to learning the rudiments of squash, and 'The Kingdom of the Khans' as it has been called, became established.

As the physical advantages of squash became better known and appreciated by the Army Council, new barracks and army centres were provided with squash courts. In the nineteen twenties the Service Clubs in London added squash courts to their amenities, and this provided a further fillip to squash in the Services. The Royal Navy were perhaps slower to build courts at their shore establishments, but even here by 1914 there was a smattering of courts at RN Bases. Afloat it was a different matter but it is worth recording that in 1920 when HRH the Prince of Wales undertook a world tour in HMS Renown a squash court was built on the upper deck in order that HRH could continue to take his exercises at one of his favourite games.

The formation of the Royal Air Force in 1917 marked an important turning point in Service squash. The Air Council has always encouraged the game amongst its personnel — at first among the officers but latterly among all ranks. Before 1939 it was routine for all new stations to have at least one squash court.

Competitive squash at the highest level started in 1925 when both the Army and the RN Championships were first played. The RAF did not commence their championship until three years later. In those days, at any rate in the two senior services, the tournaments were all officer affairs. The Championships were played at the Service clubs in London. In 1928 the Inter Service Tournament was held, and for the first nine years was monopolised by the Army, who had more opportunities of playing the game and more personnel from which to choose their teams. But the RAF enthusiasm for the game was beginning to tell and eventually in December 1937 they wrested the title from the Army. The top strings were the champions of their service and for the only time in the history of the event were brothers. B. K. Burnett, now Air Chief Marshall Sir Brian Burnett lost quite easily to his elder brother D. I. now Col Douglas Burnett (retired). The Army also won the second string tie but the keen young RAF officers won the last three strings.

After the War the Royal Navy had a good spell winning the tournament for six out of eight years between 1947 and 1954. This was the era of Seymour-Haydon, Hammond and Pellew but by 1955 all three were Commanders and there were no youngsters to take over. The Navy have never won since. In 1967 the RAF began a substantial series of wins — eight in a row. It was now the turn of the Army players to be past their best and the RAF, headed by two internationals, Peter Stokes and Don Innes were in a position to give their Service a flying start on which the lower strings were not slow to capitalise.

In the individual Service Championships, for the Army perhaps the best known player was G. O. M. Jameson. He won his first Army Championship as a Lieutenant in 1931, and his last as a Brigadier in 1946. After the War 'the Brig' as he was universally called, with his enormous reach was a difficult man to beat, made even more difficult by his refusal to give way after making a shot. In 1947 he met an opponent who was equally stubborn in this respect — Major W. H. L. Gordon; in the four games played before Jameson won there were 56 lets with considerable frustration evident on both sides. The result was an official letter from the Professionals Committee to the SRA requesting the latter to take some action to stop the increasing obstruction practised by many players, which the professionals rightly claimed was tending to ruin the game. After earnestly considering the matter the SRA Executive successfully passed the buck by instructing the Chairman of the Rules Committee to frame a rule to cover this matter. I was that unfortunate individual and for the new rule to cover obstruction I borrowed a rule from the American game which included sanctions against obstructionists by means of penalty points. Thus was born the famous Rule 17. It is worth mentioning that the words "penalty point" do not and never have featured in the wording of the rule. It was a convenient colloquialism which soon caught on. The draft I provided was accepted and duly became a rule. The professional markers were understandably reluctant to enforce it. They took the view that awarding points would antagonise those who were penalised and that this would be against the best interests of professionals. Of course, if there was an amateur referee in charge of the game the decision would be his, but in those days professional markers usually were not 'assisted' by referees.

Oscar Jameson's best years were in the early thirties and in 1933 he reached the final of the Amateur Championship, only to be soundly beaten by the great Amr Bey. A contemporary of Jameson's, C. P. Hamilton, won the Army Championship three times in the thirties and in 1934 took advantage of the temporary absence of Amr Bey to win the Amateur Championship. He was, unfortunately, killed in the War.

Since the War the most successful winner of the Army Championship has been Michael Perkins. Winning it for the first time as a lieutenant in 1953 he held the title for five consecutive years and won it altogether on eight occasions, his last win being in 1969 as a Lieutenant Colonel, a span of 16 years, which just pipped Jameson's record.

It is surprising that the advent of National Service did not produce more than one winner. This was Stuart Hicks, the Yorkshire player who took advantage of the absence abroad of better known players and past winners such as Broomfield, Perkins and de Sales la Terriere to win the Championship in 1959 for the only time. The following year Perkins was back and just managed to beat Hicks in one of the best finals for years. Hicks is the only winner who was not an officer — he was commissioned by the time he defended his title a year later. Nigel Broomfield won his first Army Championship as a Trooper but at the time was an Officer Cadet.

It would be idle to deny that in recent years, the standard of play among the top players, not only of the Army but of all the Services has declined since the halycon days of the sixties with Broomfield and Stokes. Whether this is only a temporary break remains to be seen.

The Royal Navy Championships were started in the same year as the Army Championships — 1925. In those days a great proportion of the Navy was serving afloat — and probably overseas. Leave to play in the Championships was given less readily to naval personnel than in the other Services. In 1935 half the entry for the RN Championships was composed of officers of the rank of Lieutenant Commander and above.

Before the War, the Navy's best player was Geoffrey Vavasour (now Sir Geoffrey) who won first as a Midshipman in 1932 and last in 1936 as a Sub Lieutenant. It is therefore fair to assume that his best years were lost to the War.

After the War, RN squash was dominated by Alan Seymour-Haydon. Returning to England from the Far East in 1947 he won the Championship in that year and from 1950 for five years in succession. He also played for England in the 1947/8 season and gained international honours as a member of the British Team which toured South Africa in 1955. Robin Bawtree, a product of Lancing, first won this Championship as a Cadet in 1962. Occasional service overseas limited his appearance in this event but between 1962 and 1974 he won the Championship a total of nine times, which included a run of five successive wins. Even when stationed in Home waters he was often tucked away in comparatively inaccessible ports which precluded him from regular top class competition. There seems little doubt that but for this he would have played for England.

The RAF Championships started three years after those of the other Armed Forces. In 1937 Flight Lieutenant B. K. Burnett won the event for the first time having been defeated the previous year in the final by Flight Lieutenant J. W. C. More whom he beat decisively in 1937. Burnett won the Championship on five occasions between 1937 and 1951. Sportminded young men were apt to choose the RAF in which to complete their National Service in view of the greater importance accorded to sport in that Service. Denis Hughes, a great all rounder who played for Wales at both lawn tennis and squash, was already an international when he started his National Service, and won the RAF Championship twice as an Aircraftsman. Jim Dear one of the greatest professional all-rounders of his generation won the Championship in 1945 as an LAC before being demobilised after the War. The only other player to win the RAF Championship without being commissioned was Arthur Catherine, who served as a PT Instructor. He won the Championship five times before retiring from the Service to take up a professional appointment in 1959. But the greatest player in the history of the RAF was undoubtedly Peter Stokes. Recording his first win in 1964 as a Flying Officer (which was his rank only — he was a technical officer and not a pilot) he went on to win the Championship for nine years in succession, his last in 1972 as a Squadron Leader. He was a British as well as a Welsh International and played in 58 International matches.

Although not an Armed Force, the Civil Service have held their championship since 1931. The most successful competitor was the Surrey player John Skinner with nine wins to his credit, closely followed by another Surrey player R. B. M. (now Sir Richard) King who won the Championship seven times. Colin Evans who played for Kent was the winner on four successive years 1966-69, but the best known winner was a diplomat in 1946 who went on to become Ambassador in Washington and Chief of the Foreign Office — Lord Caccia.

The Service Championships were played mainly at the Service clubs in London — the United Service Club, the Naval and Military Club and the Army and Navy Club. The RAF Championship was played for many years at the Lansdowne Club. But economy forced the Services to go to their own courts. First the Navy went to the Royal Naval College, Greenwich (at any rate for the early rounds) while the Army Championships were moved to Aldershot. The RAF Championships are now played at the RAF depot at Uxbridge.

UNIVERSITY SQUASH

For many years and at most sports "The University Match" meant Oxford v Cambridge. Nowadays with the proliferation of universities in Britain, there are many who regard Oxford and Cambridge as merely two among many, but at least the squash match between these two, the senior universities, is the oldest university squash encounter and was first played in 1925. Apart from a six year interruption from 1939 to 1944 caused by the War it has been played annually ever since. Even during the War a semi-official match took place every year alternately at Oxford and Cambridge. "Wartime Blues" were awarded but players did not sport the usual emblazoned sweaters.

Apart from these War fixtures, the University match has always been played in London, originally at Queens Club but after 1931 at one of the West End social clubs. The Public Schools had been the breeding ground of the best players and in those early days a majority of public school boys went up to Oxford or Cambridge, particularly if they were good at games. Since at most schools squash was not encouraged as a school game, it was not until a player went up to a university that he was able to indulge to the full his love of playing squash. Even then, unless likely to get his Blue, he was seldom able to receive professional coaching during term time, but members of the university teams were given plenty of opportunities of playing top class players in the matches arranged for the teams in the short season of six weeks from the middle of October to the University match at the end of November. At week-ends, clubs such as the Jesters and the Escorts sent teams to the Universities in addition to the Services, and in mid week the University teams journeyed to London to play the West End clubs, where they were afterwards well dined and wined. The chief clubs to entertain University teams in this way were the Bath, the RAC and the Junior Carlton.

The shortness of the University squash season has already been mentioned. This could not be either to the liking or to the advantage of an ambitious junior champion and may have something to do with the curious fact that no winner of the Drysdale Cup, the unofficial junior championship, has gone up to either Oxford or Cambridge since Nigel Broomfield in 1955. Squash has now become so competitive that the young squash champion cannot afford to spend the most promising three years of his squash career in this backwater, which is what the major universities are squashwise nowadays. Moreover the undergraduate of today has to work far harder at school than in the past and has less time to devote to sport, particularly if that sport is going to take him away from his university for tournaments during term time.

In recent years the British Universities Federation Championships have tended to steal the limelight and are popular with the players, possibly because women's event are included. As many as 18 universities were represented in the Mens event in 1975 and nine in the Womens. As many as 80 players compete in the mens championship and the tournament is held at a different venue every year early in December.

Starting in 1973 British Colleges Championships have also been held.

Up to the mid-sixties the standard of the University teams was remarkably high. A majority of those who played in the University match entered for the Amateur Championship which at that time was conveniently played in the Christmas vacation. The decline in the standard of play at Oxford and Cambridge in recent years has been a disturbing element in squash today. In the 1974/75 Amateur Championship only one current Blue entered. One of the causes no doubt is the decline in the number of public schoolboys who go up to these Universities, and those who do cannot afford to take the time off to go to London for matches at least once a week. The best years for University squash were from 1956-60 with the Cambridge teams of

1956 and 1957 outstanding. Two members of those teams, Nigel Broomfield and Jeremy Lyon played for England while still 'up', with the former winning the Amateur Championship while still *up*.

Although over the years neither University can claim a marked superiority over the other, success has had a habit of running in series. Thus before the War, Cambridge had a run of nine years supremacy from 1930 to 1938, nearly matched in the fifties by a run of eight successive wins. Since 1960 Oxford have been heavily in the ascendant winning 11 out of 14 contests. In these years Oxford owed a great deal to their Rhodes scholars, David Woods (1963/4/5) followed in 1968 by his younger brother Tim (1968/9), Richard Zacks (1968/69/70), Graham Macdonald (1971/72). The latter while up at Oxford was also rated top player in South Africa. Lyn Stevens, a New Zealander, also played for Oxford in 1970 and 1971.

Overseas players did not play the same prominent part in Cambridge squash during this period but earlier, in the fifties, it was usual to find players from abroad in the team. In 1953 Charles Ufford, an American, played in the team — earlier the Canadian E. R. Larsen had also won a Blue. Ufford went on to become one of the leading players in the US. Leo Melvill the present Chairman of the SRA of Southern Africa was in the Cambridge team in 1954 and 1955 while Roger Jarvis, another South African, followed him in 1958 and 1959. Jarvis might have become a top class player but soon afterwards emigrated to the US and was not heard of again squashwise. Shravan Swarup, an Indian, made the Cambridge team in 1956 and 1957 but the most unexpected overseas player to gain a Light Blue was Oon Chong Hau, a Malaysian who had gained his first Blue as a badminton player. He played squash for Cambridge in 1967 and 1968.

The fifties did not feature an overseas player in the Oxford team until 1959 when the late A. A. G. Wade, an Englishman educated at the University of Natal obtained his Dark Blue.

Facilities for playing squash at University level at both Oxford and Cambridge were abysmal. At Oxford for many years the University home matches were played on the Magdalen College courts. These had the best accommodation for spectators but suffered dreadfully from 'sweating'. More modern courts built by some of the other colleges were used in the early seventies before a University sports centre which included squash courts was built at Iffley Road and the problem has now thereby been solved.

Cambridge had Portugal Place, a University sports trust building which also catered for both varieties of fives. This had the advantage (about the only one!) of having a resident pro. For many years Mr Tabor ruled the roost and was a wonderful father figure to many generations of undergraduates. Philip Ellis, who had been pro at the West London SRC succeded him in 1959. While never a great player Ellis is a good pro and runs Portugal Place in a way of which "Mr T" would have approved.

The "Three Musketeers" of the professional game in the thirties — from the left:
'OAK' JOHNSON, CHARLES READ and CHARLES ARNOLD.

CHAPTER IX

THE MAJOR COMPETITIONS

COMPETITIONS

$\mathcal{S}$QUASH WAS for seventy years regarded as a game of enjoyment rather than of keen competition. At the public schools it was not allowed to interfere in any way with rackets and in the many private courts around the country it was used as a means of enjoying exercise when bad weather made outdoor sport impracticable, or at any rate uncomfortable. It was not until the London West End Clubs started building courts that the idea of an inter club competition was born. As usual, the Bath Club took the initiative and in October 1922 presented a challenge cup for competition between these clubs. This was the oldest inter club competition in England. In the first season the following clubs entered teams: The Bath, MCC (Lords), Princes, Queens, Royal Air Force and the RAC. In this first season the competition was won by the RAC who over the years has more wins to its credit than any other club. This is not only the premier team competition, having been played for more years than any other in England, but the standard of play in the first division was the highest in competitive squash. In the heydays of the London West End Clubs, a match was always followed by a dinner for both teams —- a most pleasant way of spending an evening.

Outside London the most competitive part of England was the North East and the oldest Area Championship is that of the North which dates back to 1924. Although this area includes Yorkshire, the mainspring of squash in the North was Northumberland where there was a small but dedicated band of players. The Newcastle SRC with three courts was the only squash club in the North, but the Northern Wayfarers was a collection of keen players with no court of their own who were prepared to go anywhere for matches, most of which were played against scratch sides on privately owned courts — a sort of Jesters of the North. Another similar club was the Yorkshire Rocks. Members of the staff of ICI at Billingham, Co Durham, played a prominent part in pioneer work for squash in the North East.

The South of England Championship started in 1927 and it is curious that both these area championships were commenced before any county championships in the area. It was three years after the founding of the Northern Area Championship that the Northumberland Championship was first played, while the Sussex Championship was not started until 1937, seven years after the first South of England Championship.

It was natural that quite early on there should have been keenness to find out who was the best professional at the game, not only by the professionals themselves but also by the club players eager to prove that theirs was the best professional. The first Professional Championship of the British Isles took place in 1920 and was on a challenge basis. (It was not until 1948 that this became a knock-out tournament.) Charles Read from Queens won in 1920 beating his challenger, A. W. B. Johnson, of the RAC. It was customary for wealthy members of the clubs to put up the side stakes for these matches, and whether it was a shortage of backers or some other cause, but Read was not challenged for this title again until 1928.

The 1925-26 season was important for in it was played the first Oxford v Cambridge match, as well as the first Royal Navy and Army Championships. This year also saw the founding of the Drysdale Cup.

The Inter County Championship was not started until 1929 a direct result of the formation of the SRA, which also had a hand in starting the Amateurs v Professionals match. Inter county competition at all sports has always created intense rivalry. At squash a number of counties raised teams before there was a county association. This was generally due to the enthusiasm of a few players who were not necessarily representative of the best players who had qualifications to play for that county. A county association, in affiliation with the clubs located in that county was obviously in a better position to choose the best team and the wish to enter a team in the Inter County Championship was frequently one of the main reasons for founding a county association.

One of the first pieces of administration by the newly formed SRA was the promotion of an Inter County Championship and the laying down of Rules to govern the tournament. Of course, a sub-committee was formed, under the Chairmanship of Sam Toyne the captain of the Yorkshire team and it was this committee which laid down the rules for qualification to play for a county.

Comparing those original qualification rules with those in force today it is perhaps surprising to see how little they have changed. Things have been made easier for service personnel but restrictions have been placed upon those players who want to change their county. It was obvious that there had to be a trophy for the Inter County Championship and in place of the conventional cup a solid silver statue of a squash player holding a racket in an indeterminate position (the model is always supposed to have been the great Sam Toyne himself) and mounted on a square plinth was presented. Yorkshire won the first Championship in 1929, but thereafter the Championship was monopolised by the South (apart from 1933 when it was again won by Yorkshire) until 1972 when it returned to Yorkshire. During that long period four counties monopolised the Championship. Surrey (15 wins), Sussex (10 wins), Middlesex (eight wins), and Kent (one win). Surrey monopolised the championship for 13 successive years from 1954 to 1966, and the architect of their success was R. B. R. Wilson. Nor was this success surprising. Surrey was the great dormitory of the squash playing types who earned their living in the City. In 1957 there were in Surrey 22 clubs containing 44 courts, against 12 similar clubs in Middlesex totalling 30 courts. Surrey also possessed the largest and most efficient county Association, built up after the war largely through the keenness of its honorary secretary, Henry Hayman, until his transplantation to the SRA in 1948, and then carried on until 1960 by another schoolmaster R. H. Baugh. One of the secrets of Surrey's success was the tremendous county spirit among the clubs and players who supported every county activity to the hilt. This county spirit was not nearly so noticeable in Middlesex were most of the players, living closer to the centre of London than in Surrey, considered themselves Londoners, and Middlesex just another team to play for.

In 1957 the number of counties entering teams for the Inter County Championship had risen to 37. Of this number 35 were English counties. The remaining two were Midlothian (Scotland) and Glamorgan (Wales). There has never so far been an inter county championship in Scotland or Wales, and these counties were the centres of squash in their countries. Soon after the resumption of the Inter County Championship after the War it was decided that the Northern Area could invite the Scottish SRA to nominate one of their counties to compete in the Northern Area while Glamorgan were similarly invited to take part in the West Midlands area.

By 1948 there were eight areas, each Area conducting its own Championship for counties in its Area. Four of these Areas held their Championship over one week-end at one venue, and these came to be known as Area Festivals. Finally, the eight winners of the Area Championships engage in a further knock-out tournament. There was naturally a great discrepancy in the strength of different counties. Some of the weaker teams got tired of being knocked out in their first match with their team often failing to win a game, let alone a tie. It was accordingly suggested that a Plate competition should be organised for those countries which had been knocked out in their first match. A handsome silver plate was presented in 1957 by Mr Christopher Campbell, the Chairman of the Inter County Championship Committee and this subsidiary tournament has given great enjoyment to a large number of medium players. The SRA was responsible for the organisation of this event and unofficially the draw was slightly 'cooked' to reduce travelling to a minimum, at any rate in the early rounds. But in 1970 the ultimate nightmare came true when Cornwall were opposed to Northumberland in the final. Commonsense prevailed, and the match was played in Birmingham!

Of the 36 English Counties which hold county Championhips, 34 started their Championships before the War. Of these most were commenced in the late thirties. Pride of place however, goes to Northumberland which started in 1927 (won by J. C. F. Simpson). Northants followed in 1932 and Derbyshire and Devon in 1933.)

It has often occurred that a County Championship has been dominated by one player, frequently for years on end. Terence Pickering won the Yorkshire Championship on 14 occasions, 13 being in successive years from 1954 to 1966 inclusive. John White won the Derbyshire Championship 13 times, 12 of which were in successive years from 1958 to 1969 inclusive. Ian Turley won his Leicestershire Championship 14 times.

It was not until 1933 that another team event appears in the records — the Sussex Inter-Club Competition. The winners for the first two years were the Rump Club. This club, famous in the annals of squash in the South of England, had no courts of its own but had the loan of courts at the Sussex County Sports Club (Withdean Stadium, Brighton, now the headquarters of the Brighton SRC), the West Sussex SRC (Chichester) and the Kensington Country Club in London. It looks as if most of the members were commuters who lived in London in mid-week and retired to Sussex for week-ends. It continued mainly owing to the enthusiasm of E. E. (Eddie) Harrison, but once his interests changed from squash to real tennis, the club quickly faded away. Apart from the Rump only three clubs have won the competition — Brighton SRC (once the Sussex County Sports Club), Middleton Sports Club, and Hove SRC.

The Wiltshire League was formed in 1937 and Service teams have played a big part in its success although the League has been won mostly by the Pythouse Club.

The Surrey League, started in 1938, quickly became after the War the largest team competition in the country. It held this position until in 1967 it was overtaken by the Lancashire and Cheshire League which had 42 teams to Surrey's 41. It is interesting to note that in the 1973/4 season the Lancashire and Cheshire teams had grown to 107 and the Surrey's to 80.

At the conclusion of the 1975/6 season there were over 1,500 teams in England playing in 33 leagues. Ten of these leagues each have 40 or more teams and the administrative work which this entails — all done by voluntary effort is yet one more example of the fine spirit which exists in the game today. It has been said with some truth that 90% of squash players play for their bi-weekly sweat and are not interested in national championships or their winners. But the number of players competing in league squash shows that there is a very healthy minority who are keen to pit their playing ability against (in many cases) total strangers. Nor must one forget the countless number of players who compete in club ladders and other club competitions.

There is one other aspect of inter club competitions which deserves mention. Team matches take up a considerable amount of court time. Even if the club gets some sort of court fees back from members of the home team, the club must be out of pocket as a result of each home match. To make matters worse many clubs run several teams — Blackburn Welfare have five teams in the Hull & District League and the club has only two courts, and there are many other clubs running four or five teams. Matches are mainly played in week-day evenings which cuts the numbers of courts available for those not playing in matches.

THE OPEN CHAMPIONSHIP

The Open Championship of the British Isles — to give it its full title, was started in 1930 on a challenge basis by the newly formed SRA. Charles Read, of Queens Club was nominated as Open Champion without having to play for it. It was not a happy choice, as by this time Read was well past his best, and he was immediately challenged by Don Butcher of the Conservative Club who beat Read easily. But two years later the arrival of Amr Bey put an end to Butcher's short reign. When Amr retired, there was only time for Dear to win it once before the outbreak of War in 1939. After the War Dear had one further win before, in 1947 the format of the Championship was changed to a knock-out competition.

The first Championship under the new rules was held at the Lansdowne Club, London in March 1948. Entries were restricted to 16 — nine professionals and seven amateurs. This meeting ground for the best amateurs and professionals caught on quickly, and the Championship soon became the most prestigious event in the squash calendar, the winner being generally accepted as the world's top player. Since those pre-War days of Amr Bey only two amateurs, Jonah Barrington and Geoff Hunt have won the Championship, and amateur runners-up have been almost as scarce. The Championship is usually played in London but for six years from 1969 onwards it was allocated to the Provinces — to the Abbeydale Club, Sheffield four times and to the Edgbaston-Priory Club in Birmingham twice. The opening of the Wembley Squash Centre brought it back to the London area. Nowadays there are large qualifying rounds and both Veterans and Vintage Championships are played at the same time as well as a Plate event.

THE AMATEUR CHAMPIONSHIP

One day in January 1923 a meeting took place at the RAC of delegates from London and Provincial Clubs interested in squash. Lord Wodehouse, who later as Lord Kimberley was to become the first President of the SRA took the Chair. It was decided by the meeting that an Amateur Championship was desirable, and should be played from April 9-14. It was also resolved that each of the Clubs represented should be entitled to enter not more than five players, and owners of private courts only one player to compete in the Championship. The court to be used for the Championship was the small court at Lords.

A committee of six being one from each of the six London Clubs (RAC, MCC, Queens, Bath, RAF and Princes) was formed to decide which ball should be used.

At a later meeting of the delegates, the Tennis & Racquets Committee recommended dimensions of a standard squash court which were considered satisfactory, and which were close to the present day dimensions.

Once the decision to hold an Amateur Championship had been taken, events moved fast. The first meeting of the sub-committee appointed at the January meeting took place only four days after they had been appointed.

The main committee which took unto itself the name of "The Squash Rackets Representative Committee" met in February to hear what the Tennis & Rackets Association wanted them to do, and started to debate points regarding the marking of the courts, but finally decided to appoint another sub-committee to deal with this problem. What a wonderful capacity the English had in those days for appointing sub-committees to deal with awkward problems! The relationship of the Representative Committee to the Tennis & Rackets Association is far from clear. For instance, the Representative Committee, having boldly fixed the date of the Amateur Championship then apparently got cold feet and wrote to the T&RA asking them when and where the entries for the Championship were to be sent, and what entrance fees were to be charged.

The sub-committee having discussed the merits of four types of ball in common use at that time, and carried out tests on three of them, decided that the ball to be used for the Championship should be the RAC standard ball. This was manufactured at the Indiarubber Gutta Percha & Telegraph Company's works at Silvertown, and was what came to be known as the Silvertown Ball.

From a letter written on February 25 by General Taylor, Secretary of the T&RA it appeared as though that body was willing to let the Representative Committee carry out the arrangements for the Championship, but reserved the right to agree or otherwise.

Only a month before the Championship was due to commence yet another sub-committee was appointed by the Representative Committee to decide what the height of the tin should be on the court in which the Championship was to be played!

One of the indeterminate aspects of the early days of the Amateur Championship was its name. In general the early championships were rightly called the Amateur Squash Rackets Championship, but a notice was circulated to all clubs in 1924 announcing that "The Open Championship of Squash Racquets" was to be played in December of that year.

It has been seen that the Public Schools were the cradle of squash in England. Loyalty to the old school has always played an important part in the Englishman's character and so inter-school rivalry among Old Boys in squash was a 'natural'. A small competition, the Queens Club Competition, organised by that club took place in 1924 and appropriately enough, taking into consideration the fact that squash started at Harrow, was won by the Old Harrovians with the Old Marlburians as runners-up. This was for teams of three-a-side. Unaccountably the tournament was never renewed and it was not until the 1934/5 season that the International Sportsmens Club put up a cup in honour of Lord Londonderry, the Club's President, for teams of Public Schools Old Boys. It was left to the teams to fix their own venues but at any rate in the early years, the matches were invariably played in London. The semi-finals and final, however, were to be played at the International Sportsmens Club who presented tankards to the winners and runners-up. The competition was organised by a sub-committee appointed by the Club which undertook the clerical work involved. Sixteen entries were received in the first year when the competition was won by the Old Etonians. Next year three more entries were received and from then on the number of teams playing rose steadily. The original rules stipulated that the competition was for Public Schools Old Boys, but with the expansion of the game to many schools which could not be classed as Public Schools it was decided to widen the scope of the competition by dropping the word 'Public'.

In the five years in which the Londonderry Cup was played prior to the War, Eton and Winchester each won twice and Harrow once. After the War by far the most successful school was Lancing, who up to the 1974/5 season, won the cup on no fewer than 17 occasions. During this period Lancing had four Internationals and, assisted by a great team spirit, managed to put their best players into court more frequently than other schools. Moreover their Internationals: J. G. A. Lyon, R. B. R. Wilson, D. R. Brazier and P. M. H. Robinson — were backed up by many other county players, and notably by D. Jude (who rather late in life than most was 'capped' by Wales) who in the ten years with which they were at their strongest, winning the cup nine times, played 38 matches in this Competition, a number only exceeded by D. R. Brazier who played 49 times in the same period. These players and the Goodwin brothers all played regularly and contributed largely to the fine record of Lancing.

The man who was chiefly responsible for generations of Lancing top class players was Sam Jagger, a master at the school, with definite and successful views on coaching. He died in 1964 after 25 years of service on the staff. His influence contributed very largely to the remarkable record of Lancing in the Londonderry Cup since the War.

Rugby was another school with a fine record. They won the cup twice running in 1960 and 1961, and were runners-up on five other occasions. Their main support came from M. A. Oddy, British and Scottish International, and other Internationals who played for them were R. M. H. Boddington and J. G. Tildesley.

In recent years the competition has been dominated by Barnard Castle, the Co Durham school. In spite of the fact that most of the members of their team live and work in the North of England, they cheerfully come to London for every round of the competition which they have won for the last seven years.

SPONSORSHIP

*S*PONSORSHIP was late in coming to squash which is perhaps hardly surprising. The wonder is that it ever came at all. The sponsor wants to see some return for his donation — and is surely entitled to it.

What, then, can a sponsor get out of squash? Most ask if the game can be televised and believe that an event sponsored by them if appearing on one of the national networks, will bring the sponsor's name before a respectably large audience. But television has fought shy of squash and even if a championship does get on the screen the opportunities of bringing the sponsor's name before the eye are very limited. The BBC would never countenance the name of the sponsor or his product being painted across, for instance, the tin. Where else? So the only advertisement the sponsor can get is to have his name incorporated in the title of the event and in the programme, or to get the media to mention as often as possible that the event is sponsored by him. Squash correspondents have been remarkably good in this way, even if sometimes it is thought good policy by the sponsor to throw a party for the Press before the event. Luckier are the sponsors who can promote a nationwide competition such as the Harp Lager, the Banbury Trophy or the Bass Charrington. In junior squash there is the Premier Products Competition. Here the name becomes known nationwide by reason of the fact that teams from all over the country take part in the various competitions.

The first sniff of sponsorship achieved by the national championships in England was the Amateur Championship in January 1971, by Tudor Processing. This was a modest effort in which a net £400 was paid towards the expenses of the Championship. But soon much bigger sums came to be offered and both the Open and Amateur Championships were sponsored by Benson & Hedges starting in the 1971/2 season with sums up to £5,000 being donated. The sums donated continued to grow and the 1978 British Open Championship was sponsored to the tune of £15,000 by Avis Rent-a-Car.

With events open to professionals there is no limit to the amount which can be absorbed as prize money, but with the amateur events the position is more complicated. The SRA set a limit of £50 for the value of any prize which may be accepted by an amateur but with inflation this sum has been increased to £100. This is over and above the value of a challenge trophy which the winner keeps for only one year. There have been occasions when the sponsor has contributed towards the air fares of a player coming from abroad, but the bulk of the money goes to paying a daily rate which may be as high as £8 out of which the chief players have to pay their own living expenses. Most sponsors also like to donate a challenge trophy bearing their own name and, of course, there is the inevitable party after the final of the event.

It is instructive to analyse the various sponsoring firms. Of the 30 sponsors of various events in the UK and Ireland in the years 1971-74 the following table shows the diversity of the firms who have thought fit to put some money into the game:

General commercial	9
Smokes	6
Squash (court makers, clothes)	5
Drink	4
Insurance	3
Finance	3

The general commercial category embraced such products as bookmakers, watches, photographic accessories, etc.

There was some heartsearching at the SRA about the propriety of allowing sponsorship on behalf of hard liquor and smokes, but the general concensus of opinion was that the fact that a sponsor wanted to help the game by pouring money into it did not necessarily mean that the governing body or the tournament concerned endorsed the product.

The growth of sponsorship was not lost on the SRA and while the Annual Report for 1969/70 stated: "plans are well advanced for a considerable increase of this very acceptable form of encouragement to the game", the Annual Report for the following year stated: "steps were taken, however, to keep sponsorship under the control of the

Association'', and at the Annual General Meeting in September 1971 a new rule of the Association was introduced which made it obligatory for any intending sponsor of a squash activity in England (but not including events under the control of the WSRA) to obtain the prior approval of the SRA. Increasing sponsorship was later looked upon as a minor gold mine and the SRA in 1972 added to the Rule by laying down that the sponsors should pay to the Association a sum equivalent to 15% of the total sponsored monies.

Sponsorship of women's events has not been on the same scale as that enjoyed by mens competitions. Mention should be made, however, of BP who sponsored the Women's Championships during the years when it was played at the Company's sports ground at Sydenham. In addition to giving the prizes, the sponsors made free the use of the courts and gave a party after the final for all and sundry.

In other parts of the world squash has not been sponsored on the same scale as in England. The International Championships in New Zealand were the first of these to be sponsored (the SRA had failed to find a sponsor for the 1969 International Championships played in England). The Rothman's Sports Foundation contributed a total of NZ$3,800 towards the expenses of the Championship. In 1973 the International Championships in South Africa were sponsored chiefly by the Louis Luyt Breweries, but valuable assistance was given by Cabana Beach (an offshoot of Anglo American Corporation).

In Australia the main championships have been sponsored by a soft drinks firm and the Singapore Championships have been also sponsored.

In Europe the first European Championships which were held in Edinburgh in 1973 were sponsored by the Target Trust Group, but in the following year Pilkington Bros of England, manufacturers of the glass back walls, agreed to sponsor the championship for three years.

In 1974 and 1975 the number of tournaments receiving sponsored assistance rose fantastically and by 1976 there were few tournaments in the fixture list which were not sponsored, some firms such as Benson & Hedges which has supported the Amateur and Open Championships for some years withdrew, but there was no lack of firms willing to take their place. However, in 1976 the SRA had some difficulty in finding adequate sponsorship for the Amateur International Championships played in England that year. But the 1976/77 fixture list contained nearly 60 sponsored tournaments.

Few companies have contributed to squash on such a large scale as Pakistan International Airways. For some years the most promising amateur players in Pakistan were taken on the company's payroll and spent most of their time when in that country in 'squash camps' when their sole duty appeared to be to play squash against each other. An exception, however, is the case of Aftab Jawaid who has for many years worked in the company's freight department at Karachi. It may well be that his success at the game was a considerable factor in persuading the company to become involved in squash. Nor did they limit their sponsorship activities to Pakistan and in 1975 they sponsored the British Amateur Championship. The PIA Chairman, Air Marshal Nur Khan, entered enthusiastically into his company's squash activities, and he was largely instrumental in promoting what the Pakistanis were pleased to call the World Cup for the Hashim Khan Trophy, a tournament in the stifling heat of Karachi in April 1976 (no air conditioning in the courts) for amateurs and pros for a team event as well as an individual tournament.

This is all the more surprising in view of the fact that squash is not a popular game in Pakistan. There are only 120 courts and squash was considered a costly game and was therefore not played by many. It was restricted to the cantonment area.

Sponsorship is now part of the normal sporting life and squash sponsorship, if slow to start, now plays an invaluable part in the game the world over.

COMMERCE AND SQUASH

The squash boom inevitably attracted Big Business. The involvement of commerce in the game took two forms — building and ownership of squash centres, and sponsorship.

Although a number of clubs were owned by small companies it was not until 1966 that the first large scale operation was launched by ABC Cinemas, who planned to build squash complexes in the car parks of some of its cinemas — the first one at Walton-on-Thames, Surrey. The start was a modest club of three courts. Its immediate success not only encouraged the company to add a further two courts at Walton, but to enlarge the scope of its operations by building other squash centres, first at Richmond (Surrey), and then at South Kensington. The continued success of the operation led to an increasing number of clubs being built in various parts of the country so that in a few years there were over 20 such clubs operating successfully.

The success of EMI which had taken over ABC Cinemas, led to other companies mounting similar operations, and in particular a property company, Town & Country, which not only built clubs in England but erected in 1974 an absurdly expensive club in the heart of Paris — it was alleged to have cost £800,000 for six courts. The collapse of the property market in England involved this company and most of the English clubs have been sold off. But the Paris Club is still successfully operating. Other companies such as Gunnerslade which opened four clubs in various parts of England and which were hit by rising building costs and interest rates, were forced to call in a Receiver, although the clubs were all doing good business, and have since been snapped up by other companies.

144

COMMERCIAL DEVELOPMENT

In Australia where commercial court owning was highly developed years before the phenomenon appeared in England, the court owners formed their own association in New South Wales in the early sixties. Unfortunately relations between that body and the SRA of Australia quickly became strained and remained so for a number of years. This was largely a personality clash and eventually relations improved and the court owners worked harmoniously with the SRAA for the solution of their many mutual problems.

The growth of commercial squash in Great Britain in the late sixties led to the SRA encouraging the formation of a court owners organisation in this country which, to quote from the SRA Annual Report for 1969/70 "will not only benefit its members but will also actively co-operate with the SRA to the mutual benefit of both parties". The SRA gave the Court Owners Association its official backing in 1971 by granting it representation on the Council. It was appropriate that Mr. J. C. Jeffryes the owner of the Ealing Squash Courts, perhaps the oldest commercial squash courts in this country, should be appointed Chairman and Acting Secretary. But the COA was a weakling. Perhaps the members were too busy trying to make their courts pay; perhaps Mr Jeffryes had not the time to devote to working up enthusiasm but the fact remains that it did very little.

But in 1973 the proprietors were stung by the efforts of the SRA to increase the affiliation fee for clubs to £25 per court. Up to 1971 the affiliation fee had been 10/6d per court, payment for which was the responsibility of the county associations, which often added a further 10/6d in order to finance themselves. In 1971 the fee was raised to £5 per court but when only two years later the SRA raised the fee to £25 per court the proprietory clubs rebelled. Mr Rex Guppy whose (at that time) 10 court club at Basildon (Essex) was one of the largest clubs in the country led the revolt and in June 1973 circularised all proprietory squash clubs in the UK inviting them to become founder members of the "British Squash Rackets Federation", a title subsequently amended to "British Squash Rackets Proprietors Federation". The response was enthusiastic and the new organisation which took over the Court Owners Association came into being on July 24, 1973, at a meeting at Hemel Hempstead. Mr Guppy in his opening remarks made it clear that it would not be the intention of the Federation to compete in "any shape, size, or form with the SRA".

The main discussion at the meeting centred round what proprietorial clubs would be willing to pay by way of an affiliation fee to the SRA. Many of those present were dissatisfied with the services given by the SRA in return for affiliation, and by the inefficiency of the SRA with particular reference to the collection of club affiliation fees. Finally it was agreed that the Federation members would be prepared to pay a donation to the SRA of £10 per court per member for 1973, the figure to be reviewed in the following years in the light of development progress of the SRA and the BSRPF.

Mr Guppy was elected Chairman of the Federation. Mr F. Cockerill, of County Squash Rackets Ltd, Vice-Chairman, and Mr Jeffryes, Treasurer. Many schemes were proposed by which the Federation could aid the proprietors and their clubs, and there can be no doubt that the Federation got off to a splendid start.

The SRA could not be expected to agree to the Federation's terms and a long wrangle commenced. The members of the BSRPF withheld their affiliation fees, and the clubs represented were officially disaffiliated and not allowed to take part in county leagues, nor were their courts allowed to be used for SRA fixtures such as county championship matches. But in a great number of cases, the harsh threats of the SRA were completely ignored, and many of the sanctions imposed were not carried into effect.

However, in July 1975 a truce was reached when, as a result of intensive discussions which had been taking place during the 1974-5 winter between the SRA and the BSRPF compromise proposals were placed before an Extraordinary General Meeting of the SRA and carried by a 94% majority. New affiliation fees were agreed under which the maximum a club could pay was £125 per annum, and a sub-committee was set up consisting of members of the SRA and the BSRPF to look into any further anomalies which might exist. As a result, all the proprietorial clubs became affiliated to the SRA once more.

CHAPTER X

CLUB SQUASH

THE SQUASH CLUB

*T*HE CLUB is a recognised English institution which has been copied in many overseas countries. It has been said that wherever two or three Englishmen find themselves together away from their home country, the first thing they do is to form a club. Roughly speaking clubs are either social or sporting. The first social clubs were formed in the London Coffee houses and had a strongly political flavour. The sporting clubs were formed for the purpose of providing facilities, practice and competition at a particular sport or sports. The MCC is one of the oldest and best known sporting clubs.

In the early days of squash the first clubs to take up squash in the London area were Princes and Queens, which had been established for a number of sports long before they took up squash. When we come to endeavour to establish which is the oldest club started purely for squash, the answer would appear to be, surprisingly, the Aberdeen SRC which was founded in 1909. At that time there were few clubs with squash courts in the North and there is no record of the club playing any other squash club untill the early thirties when the club sent a team to oppose the Northern Wayfarers Club at Newcastle-on-Tyne, and in the following year visited Edinburgh to play the Edinburgh Academicals Club at Raeburn Place. The Club enjoyed the use of two courts at Hardgate but during the War years the landlords required the courts for other uses and they were never again used for squash.

147

But if the Aberdeen Club successfully lays claim to the title of the oldest squash club in Britain, they are well beaten by a club in Canada which was founded in 1905. The Toronto Racquet Club opened in that year and was founded solely for the purpose of playing squash and affords almost no facilities other than that. Although playing was suspended during the 1914-18 War, the club was able to carry on in the next War without shutting down. New premises were acquired in the nineteen fifties and the club is still going strong.

The social side of squash has always been of the greatest importance and accounts for the large number of private courts up and down the country. The squash club as such was a product of the first boomlet of squash in the early thirties. Even at that stage squash was considered a fairly snobbish game. Roy McKelvie, writing in the 'Daily Express', in 1932, baldly stated: "Squash is not a game for democracy". However wrong that view may be today, few were prepared to question it in 1931 and it is therefore all the more remarkable that in that year one Gilbert Jacob had the foresight to erect a 4 court complex in a central position at Ealing, on the Western outskirts of London. Moreover, these were public courts, open to all who wanted to play. In connection with the courts was founded at the same time the Ealing Squash Club the members of which, for a modest subscription, were able to use a bar and obtain refreshments and, even more important, to play the game competitively. Many famous players including Jonah Barrington and Richard Boddington first played their London competition matches as members of this club which during the 45 years of its existence has won the Banbury Trophy, the Cumberland and Coolhurst Cups and many other honours. Today the courts, now grown to six, are still flourishing and claim to be the oldest public squash centre in the world.

The London West End Social clubs were the first clubs to add squash courts to their amenities and have played a unique part in the history of the game. The oldest courts were those at Princes Club and the RAC whose courts were built before the 1914-18 War. Princes was not strictly speaking a West End Social Club and was from its earliest days a sporting club like Queens. Its premises were in Knightsbridge and the two squash courts were believed to have been the oldest in London. The Club was closed down before the 1939 War. The RAC in Pall Mall built two courts in about 1913. After that War two more were added, but because of the lack of space they were narrower than laid down in the official specifications. The Centre Court there could, at a pinch, accommodate nearly 100 spectators and from 1958 to 1961 the Amateur Championship was played at that club. In 1948 it was decided to reconstruct the second, third and fourth courts as a result of which the second and third courts were rebuilt to a standard width, and the fourth court was converted into an American court, which is narrower than the British court.

The two courts at the old Bath Club in Dover Street were built in

1922 and were the scene of the Amateur Championship from 1923 to 1938. These courts were destroyed by fire in 1943.

After the Great War, Queens were first in the field with two courts in 1919, followed by the Conservative (2) in 1920. The MCC built one court which was very large (the size of the standard court was not laid down until 1922) and it was here that the first Amateur Championship was played in 1922.

In the late twenties and early thirties many social clubs built squash courts and it is worth putting on record that in 1938 the following West End Social Clubs had squash courts, with the number of courts each club had in brackets.

Army & Navy Club, Pall Mall (1)
Bachelors Club, South Audley Street (2)
Bath Club, Dover Street (2)
Caledonian Club, St. James Square (2)
Conservative Club, St. James Street (2)
Guards Club, Brook Street (now Bath Club) (2)
Hurlingham Club, Fulham (2)
International Sportsmans Club, Upper Grosvenor Street (4)
Junior Carlton Club, Pall Mall (3)
Junior United Service Club, Charles Street (1)
Ladies Carlton Club, Grosvenor Place (3) Including a doubles court.
Lansdown Club, Berkeley Square (4)
Marlborough Club, Pall Mall (1)
Marylebone Cricket Club, St Johns Wood (3)
Naval & Military Club, Piccadilly (2)
Public Schools Club, Piccadilly (2)
Princes Club, Knightsbridge (3)
Queens Club, West Kensington (4)
Royal Aero Club, Piccadilly (1)
Royal Air Force Club, Piccadilly (2)
Royal Automobile Club, Pall Mall (4)
Royal Thames Club, Knightsbridge (1)
Union Club, Carlton House Terrace (2)
United Hunts Club, Upper Grosvenor St. (1)
United Service Club, Pall Mall (2)
United University Club, Suffolk Street (1)

It is a sad commentary that 16 of the above 27 clubs have had either to close down or to amalgamate with other clubs, and that 4 of the remaining 11 clubs have lost between them five courts. The only courts built since 1939 are two courts at the Oxford and Cambridge with which the United University Club amalgamated in 1973. The Junior Carlton Club was rebuilt in 1967 and the three courts at the old club were reduced to two, but these too have now vanished with the club.

The Lansdowne Club has always catered for the younger set and in addition to squash has a swimming pool and fencing salon. Under the enlightened leadership of Lord Aberdare a court with a large gallery was built in 1933 and opened in 1935. The gallery originally contained 144 seats which with side and back standing raised the gallery capacity to about 200, the largest in London.

It was the venue of the chief SRA Championships for a number of years from 1946 onwards, but relations between the SRA and the Club were variable, and from 1958 to 1961 the Amateur and Open Championships migrated to the RAC before returning to the Lansdowne. The Open Championship left London in 1968 for the Provinces, and the Amateur Championship was not played at the Lansdowne after 1971.

Squash clubs can be divided into two classes — those which are owned collectively by the members, and those which are privately owned, and from which the owner expects to make a profit, and quite probably his livelihood. In the early days most clubs belonged to the former category, but among the first privately owned courts were the Ealing courts already referred to, and the Wanstead Squash Club in Essex.

The involvement in squash of large commercial companies has been the most significant development in squash in the period commencing in the late sixties. First in the field was Associated British Cinemas. At Walton-on-Thames in Surrey this company owned a cinema with an unusually large car park. In an effort to make the car park more productive the company decided to erect therein a squash club which initially comprised three squash courts. Before committing themselves the company posted several thousand reply paid cards to residents enquiring about the desirability or otherwise of having a squash club in Walton. Encouraged by the replies, ABC went ahead and the club was opened in June 1966. Such was the success of this venture that two additional courts were added in 1968, and further clubs were built in the same year by the company adjoining their cinemas at Richmond (Surrey) and Maidenhead (Berkshire). The Priory Lawn Tennis and Squash Club at Blackheath in Kent wich had opened in 1937 was purchased by the company in 1968 and the number of squash courts increased. The activities of ABC (later absorbed into the EMI empire) continued to expand, and a separate company was formed in 1969 to take over the squash activities of the parent company.

By 1977 nineteen clubs were owned by this group. Another group with clubs at Northwood, Hemel Hempstead, Peterborough, Watford and Stevenage was next on the scene and since 1970 a large number of companies has seen fit to climb on the bandwaggon. A large majority of courts built since 1971 have been commercially owned. Insofar as they have catered for the demand for squash facilities, they have rendered excellent service to the game, but there can be no doubt that they have increased the cost of playing squash which was always regarded as a cheap game. This is not to state that large profits have been made by the developing companies. The facilities provided off court are far greater than in the old clubs, with comfortable lounges, TV sets and light refreshments and often billiards, in addition to the universal bar. Moreover the profits had to include interest to the shareholders or the banks who had provided the capital, whereas in the Members Clubs no profit was budgeted for and if made was ploughed back into the club.

WEST END CLUBS

The London West End Social Clubs have always played an important part in squash, and the game in London was born in these clubs. It was a natural follow through to squash played in country houses, the Services and the schools. The first clubs to build courts were the RAC whose courts were built as far back as 1911. The first court built by the MCC at Lords was in 1922, and was immediately used for the first Amateur Championship.

The advantages of quick exercise after a day's work in the City quickly became apparent and more and more clubs decided to build courts. Some were built on the roof, as at the Junior Carlton, while others, as at the RAC were built in the basement. Finding space in an existing building was not always easy, for most clubs were already built before squash became a 'must'. Clubs found that the possession of squash courts was a good recruiting counter with which to attract young men arriving from the universities to work in London, and many offered membership at reduced fees for younger members. The salad days of the London social clubs were between the Wars. Many of them never recovered from the 1939/45 War. The squash courts of some, such as the Bath, the Ladies Carlton and Queens were destroyed in the War. In other cases in the years following the second War hard times hit Clubland and a number closed down — these included the Bachelors, Badminton, Conservative, International Sportsmens, United Service, Marlborough, Princes (which in fact closed down before the War), Royal Aero (which itself had taken over the premises of the Cavendish Club when that club closed down in 1931), Union etc. Then again some clubs either moved to new premises or were rebuilt on the same site, which involved either loss of courts or at least a reduction in their numbers. In 1936 there were 25 West End Social Clubs with their own courts, 53 in number. By 1972 the number of clubs had fallen to 11 with 27 courts.

In recent years very few new courts have been built in West End Social Clubs. The Junior Carlton, which rebuilt their club on the same site, lost the three courts which were on the roof of the old building, but built two courts in the reconstructed club, but these were lost when the club premises were closed in 1977. The United University had two roof courts in their premises in Suffolk Street. The club amalgamated with the Oxford and Cambridge Club in 1973 and as part of the reconstruction of much of the premises of the latter to cater for the larger joint membership. two squash courts were built. At the Hurlingham Club two new courts were added in 1973 bringing their total number of courts to four. The question might well be asked — is Hurlingham a West End Social Club? Its status as such rests largely on the fact that it has for many years competed in the Bath Club Cup which is normally open only to West End Social Clubs. Queens was a founder member of the Cup and its status is so similar to that of Hurlingham that the latter were successful in their application to join the competition in 1950.

The Bath Club Cup

The many amalgamations and takeovers in London's clubland in the past few years have had a serious effect on the Bath Club Cup. Started in 1922 — which makes ħ the oldest league at least in this country, the competition thrived during the years when many of the West End clubs were adding squash courts. In 1929 a second division was formed and in the following year a third. In 1936 there were 18 clubs in the three divisions. The following clubs have dropped out since then: Conservative, Princes, International Sportsmens, Bachelors, Royal Aero, Union, Army & Navy, Caledonian, Badminton, New University and United University. Of these only the Army & Navy and the Caledonian still survive without courts. Clubs playing in the competition now which were not playing in 1936 are the Lansdowne, Hurlingham, HAC and the Cavalry.

For the first two seasons after the War the competition was played on a knock-out basis but in 1948 the-league system was reintroduced. The ten years after this saw the Bath Club Cup at its zenith when every aspiring first class player felt that he had to take part in the competition to get regular top class opposition. The Bath Club Cup has always been for teams of three so that it was the more difficult to get into a Bath Club Cup team than into the five-a-sice teams in the Cumberland Cup. As hard times overtook London Clubland it became necessary to raise subscriptions and this made it less attractive for younger members in spite of the more advantageous terms often offered to younger members by many clubs. Cumberland Cup clubs, although lacking the social standing of their West End brethren, had much lower subscriptions and this more than anything else resulted in a gradual shift of the top players to their ranks and away from the delights of the West End.

Before the War, in more leisurely times it was the custom to start Bath Club Cup matches as early as 4.00 p.m., but after the War the executive classes worked harder and matches seldom started before 5.30 p.m. at the earliest. The clubs in the first division started the practice of dining the visiting team after matches, the cost of which was often borne by the home club. The best dinners were those given by the Bath and the Junior Carlton clubs. At the end of the season it was customary for the winning First Division club to play a match against drawn from other clubs in the First Division, and this was followed by a dinner given by the Club at which the cup was presented by a senior member of the Bath Club Committee.

A not unimportant reason for the diminution of the status of the Bath Club Cup was the action of the Press in withdrawing publicity by omitting to print the results of the matches. Blame for this should not be laid entirely at the door of the Press. Matches tended to last longer in the sixties and it was frequently 9.00 p.m. or later before matches were finished and the result phoned through to the agencies, too late for publication in the following morning's papers. It was this late finish which was also responsible for the decline in the dining habit, many clubs having a rule that all dinners had to be started before 8.30 p.m. owing to staff costs.

In the sixties, a number of clubs were allowed into the competition which did not have courts of their own. Thus, in the 1965/6 season we find five clubs — Public Schools, Guards, East India and Sports, Cavalry and Airborne, which all had to find other West End Clubs in which to play their matches. This resulted in the production of the Bath Club Cup fixture list, organised by the Bath, becoming an increasingly complex operation. Thursday nights, traditionally Bath Club Cup nights, became reserved only for the first division clubs. Others had in many instances to spill over to Wednesday nights. The Naval and Military Club were at one time the 'home club' of no less than five clubs, and even with play in this competition restricted to one court, the members of the host club had a lean time booking courts for friendly games.

In 1963 the Lansdown Club initiated the Lansdowne Trophy which was open to clubs taking part in either the Bath Club Cup or the Cumberland Cup and was on a Knock-out basis for teams of five. This never caught on and after six years was discontinued.

FAMOUS CLUBS

Abbeydale Park, Sheffield

Cricket, hockey, rugby and football were played by different clubs but with one ground at Abbeydale Park, on the outskirts of Sheffield. In 1933, 150 playing members of the other clubs agreed to put up £10 each to start a squash club and three courts with changing rooms were built. After the War, membership rapidly increased and by 1954 sufficient funds had been generated to build a fourth court— the first squash court to be built in England after the War. A fifth court followed in 1959 and a sixth in 1962. Finally in 1971 the club opened the first complete glass back-walled court built at a cost of £31,000 all of which money had been generated by the Squash Club. The driving force in much of this development was the founder, the late Mr. Robert Hargreaves, while Mr. John Willows the Secretary of the parent of all the sports clubs at Abbeydale, the Sheffield Amateur Sports Club, and himself a Yorkshire county squash player for many years, efficiently organised for many years until his retirement all the important squash events staged there. These included five Open Championships and many other important fixtures in the squash calendar.

The standard of play in the club has always been high and the club reached the final of the National Club Championship three times between 1909 and 1975. By the latter year the squash membership had reached 1,100 of which 150 are women and 200 juniors. The club has benefitted from having a series of top class professionals including Jack Giles, Khan Din and Ahmet Safwat.

The Rump

In the thirties, easily the most famous squash club outside London was the Rump. This was a Sussex club founded in 1930 by E. E. Harrison, who played squash (and cricket) for Sussex for many years immediately prior to the War and was a winner of the South of England Championship and many other squash tournaments. A co-founder was A.R. (now Sir Alexander) Glen. Although many of its members — there were 542 in 1936 — were from all over the country, the Club was primarily a Sussex Club. It had no courts of its own, and was therefore a roving club similar to the Jesters and the Escorts. Famous Sussex players such as Sam Jagger and Edward Snell, both alas now dead, served on the Committee and in 1936 the Club's fixture list contained 127 matches. Like all other squash clubs of this nature the Rump died in the War and Mr. Harrison did not feel like reconstituting it afterwards. By that time he had become Honorary Secretary of the Sussex SRA and that body adopted the Rump Club tie as the tie to be worn by those who had been awarded their Sussex County Badge.

Edgbaston — Priory

Squash in the Birmingham area was dominated by two lawn tennis clubs in Edgbaston — the Priory LTC and the Edgbaston Cricket and Lawn Tennis Club. The Priory, founded in 1875 was the senior club by three years. It was not until 1934 that two squash courts were added to the amenities of the club. The number of squash members was limited to 135. The club continued to prosper but no more courts were built, and this was the position when in 1963 the wooden pavilion was totally destroyed by fire. The squash courts had been saved and one of them was pressed into service as a club-room and bar.

The Edgbaston club, only half a mile away from Priory, opened two squash courts, also in 1934, with a third added in 1956. Cricket faded out in 1903 and in 1930 the club was renamed the "Edgbaston Lawn Tennis Club". Squash played a more important part in the club than at the Priory and representative matches such as the Amateurs v. Professonals were played on the club courts. After the fire at Priory it was decided to amalgamate the two clubs on the Priory site with a new pavilion and four more squash courts, making six in all. The new club was opened in 1967. In 1972 a further squash court with a gallery able to accommodate 100 spectators was added and in 1974 two more courts were completed, one of which was capable of being converted into a gallery for the other.

The new club at once became the best appointed squash club in the Midlands. In 1970 the Open Championship was played there while in the previous year the club was used as the headquarters for the team event of the Amateur International Championships. The late Mr. Arthur Boyse, the squash Chairman collected an enthusiastic hard working and efficient team which has organised these and other important tournaments which have been held at the club.

From 1970 to 1976 the late Nazrullah Khan was the squash professional and this contributed largely to the high standard of play. This has been especially noticeable in recent years among the Women.

Jesters

Perhaps the most famous squash club in the world — and it hasn't got a single squash court! Founded in 1929 as a Rugby Fives Club the original fixture list contained one squash fixture. While in the mid-thirties the Club played over 200 squash matches each season, the number has now been considerably reduced and nowadays the Club plays 86 squash matches and another 113 Rugby Fives, Eton Fives, Tennis and Rackets fixtures. The Club has always specialised in sending teams to play schools and 17 fixtures against school sides in addition to over 50 similar matches in the other games played by the Club are on the fixture list. There are nearly 1,000 members of the Club in England and branches have been established in Canada, the USA and South Africa. The Founder of the Club, Mr. J. F. Burnet was for many years a bursar at Cambridge and still takes an active interest in the Club. Membership which is only by invitation, has always been considered a great honour and prowess at any of the games played is by no means the only qualification. The reputation of the Club is so high that although it can never play a 'home ' match, squash organisations are always keen to play the Jesters. The Club does however entertain overseas teams visiting this country and plays host to tours here arranged by its overseas branches.

In 1979 the Club celebrated its golden jubilee.

GALLERIES AND GLASS BACK WALLS

When the sub committee of the Tennis and Rackets Association laid down in 1922 the dimensions of the court, which have remained unaltered since then, nothing was mentioned about the gallery which, being outside the court was no concern of theirs. Nor have the SRA or the ISRF thought fit to lay down anything on the subject. Oviously there had to be a gallery, however small, to house the marker and the referee, both officials mentioned in the Rules of the game and it is perhaps odd that the rules do not contain some reference to where these important officials (at least in competitive squash) should perform their duties.

Squash is pre-eminently a participant sport. Even national championships, at least to start with, were played in courts with little provision for spectators. At the old Bath Club in Dover Street where the Amateur Championship was played from 1923 to 1938, not more than 50 spectators could be accommodated. At this time the largest gallery in England was at the Royal Automobile Club where the main court could at any rate in theory hold 100. Here there were individual seats for 16 spectators in the front row with tiered benches behind and on the right hand side, with chairs on the left hand side. But those in the back row at the sides could see less than half of the court. In 1933 was commenced at the Lansdowne Club the building of what came to be known as the Bruce Court (the family name of Lord Aberdeen who as Chairman of the Club was responsible for its construction). At the back of this court there were twelve rows of seats which could accommodate 144 spectators. Over the left hand side of the court there was standing room for a further twenty and with further standing room at the back of the seats, nearly 200 could be crowded in.

Outside London there was great rivalry between the Abbeydale Club at Sheffield and the Edgbaston Priory Club at Birmingham. In 1962 a sixth court was added at the former club which was the finest in the country at that time and could hold 100 spectators. Meanwhile the amalgamation of the Edgbaston and the Priory Lawn Tennis Clubs at Birmingham was marked by the construction of a large galleried court from which over 100 spectators (mostly standing) could watch the play while another — the Boyse Court (named after the Club's squash chairman) was added with a gallery which could hold 200.

Overseas several larger galleries were built. The Wanderers Club in Johannesberg had a court which with additional scaffolding erected for important matches could hold 400. The Victoria SRA squash complex in Melbourne was a championship court into the galleries of which 500 spectators can be crammed. But in Cairo there were two courts with what was claimed to be seating for 500. with the same number being accommodated at the Alexandria Sporting Club.

There is a court at Salisbury, Rhodesia which can accomodate over

600 spectators which is at the moment the largest gallery in the world.

The coming of the glass back wall marked an important step forward in spectator comfort, even if it has not yet led to any significant increase in the numbers of spectators accommodated. It is interesting to note that the idea of transparent built squash courts had been put forward in 1938. An advertisement in the Squash Rackets Annual of that year stated: "The new invention allows of a direct perfect view of play for a large audience frm the level of the court. A semi-transparent panel is let into the wall of a court, and through this the details of a game can be easily followed. The panel is rendered opaque on the playing side by a special finely woven while gauze behind the plate glass". I have been unable to come across any record of a court of this nature having been built and it is probable that the outbreak of War effectively killed the construction of such courts. The god parent of the glass wall was undoubtedly television. Televison of squash was already flourishing in Australia in the middle sixties but the camera was usually placed so far behind the court that it was difficult to follow the small black ball at such a distance.

In 1965 a British Womens team toured Australia and took part in the Australian Womens Championship which was played at Hobart, Tasmania. They brought back with them reports of a glass panel which had been inserted into the door leading into the court and through which many of the matches had been televised. Details of the glass were readily made available by the Australians to the SRA, and in 1967 a glass panel was constructed in a new court at the Birkenhead Squash Club. This was almost the whole width of the court and about four feet deep.

Generally speaking glass courts are of two types. The earlier ones were about ten feet high, above which there was the traditional gallery, which gave a two tiered effect, the 'stalls' looking into the court through the glass and the 'dress circle' looking directly into the court. Subsequently the free standing glass wall was developed wich resulted in the number of rows of seats being limited simply by the increasing distance from the players.

A number of courts have two tiers at the sides of the court — a good example of this is at the Edinburgh Sports Club and another is the Victoria SRA championship court in Melbourne. But not more than two rows of each tier can see enough of the court to make watching worthwhile.

In 1971 there was a proposal for an all glass court which would be portable and which could be quickly erected in any indoor arena such as the Albert Hall. Sponsorship was promised for this novelty once a prototype had been erected. This was always promised but nothing came of the idea once it had been admitted that each time the court was erected the cost would be £1,500.

CHAPTER XI

THE INTERNATIONAL AMATEUR CHAMPIONSHIPS

$\mathcal{A}$S AUSTRALIA in agitating for an International Federation had been motivated largely by a desire to secure at least a bite at the World Amateur Championship cherry, it was natural that the newly formed ISRF should award the first International Amateur Championship to that country. There was considerable discussion on the subject of the title and Australia and other countries were hoping that the event would be called the World Championship. Wiser counsels pointed out that there would be an outcry from America if this title were adopted and it was finally decided to call the event the International Amateur Championships. This did not stop the Press from referring to the World Championships and there was very little the Federation could do about it.

While a team event was considered the more important, it was recognised that an individual event should be included and this has given all the host countries the opportunity of spreading the Championships among at least two venues. The rules governing the International Championships laid down that the team event should be played first, but after the third Championships in New Zealand, when most of the Canadians and some others did not bother to wait for the Plate tournament of the individual event, it was recommended that the order should be reversed, in order to get as large an entry as possible for the Plate. The next Championships were played in South Africa and the governing body of that country immediately appealed.

158

The venues for the Championships here were to be Johannesburg and Durban. It was feared that those knocked out early in the individual event would, were it to be played in Johannesburg, immediately make tracks for Durban in order to get longer acclimatisation at sea level after playing in the rarefied atmosphere of Johannesburg. Thus the Plate event would suffer and those players who would be free to go early to Durban would get an unfair advantage. This seemed logical and permission was given for the ISRF recommendation to be ignored.

So the first Championships got underway in Australia in 1967 with the Team event played first at a number of clubs in the suburbs of Sydney. The Australians were hot favourites to win which they did without losing a tie. Their team consisted of, Ken Hiscoe, Geoff Hunt and Dick Carter, with Cam Nancarrow as reserve. The British team centred on Jonah Barrington, who was also captain. This was a mistake. Jonah is always a 100% competitor and his rigorous and sometimes unconventional methods of training were apt to conflict with the social duties of a captain; it was usually the former which prevailed. The British were recognised by Australia as being their chief rivals and as such the final match of the tournament was between these two countries. This unofficial form of seeding was considered a good thing and when a few years later Australia and Britain played their match early on, there was criticism that once the winner of this match was known, the result of the Championship became a foregone conclusion, and interest waned.

But to return to 1967, one innovation was the televising of the matches. The difficulties of the TV producer and crew were not exactly diminished by the variety of clubs and courts in which the matches were played. None of the clubs in Sydney had glass doors and the most usual positions of the cameras were to have one in the middle of the gallery, and two others situated on either side wall about five feet from the back wall. These latter were to pick up the play in the opposite back corner with the gallery camera doing the main job of catching the play in the front of the court. During the week or ten days of the team event the same TV crew televised one match each evening and it was noticeable that the quality of the television improved with time and experience. When the Championships moved on to Melbourne for the individual event, only the final was televised and by a different crew. Although a glass panel had been inserted into the door of the court no use was made of this for television (possibly because steps to the door made it impossible to give a firm stand for the camera) and the camera was placed at the back of the gallery — much too far from the court to see the ball.

In order to cut down expense, both for countries travelling to the Championships and for the host country in providing board and lodging for the teams, it has been decided at the outset that teams should be of three only, with one travelling reserve. This resulted in the ties being played on one court at each club. As the matches did not start until 8.00 p.m. it was frequently 11.00 p.m. before play finished and then followed the inevitable bun-worry. There were understandable complaints from some teams that they were getting to bed too late!

Both at Sydney and Melbourne all the teams were accommodated in the same hotel. The Australians set a high standard of hospitality and it was difficult to fault the arrangements made for the entertainment of the visiting teams.

The Individual event was mainly notable for the defeat of top seeded Jonah Barrington by Cam Nancarrow in the semi-finals. It had been said that Barrington did not like playing a fellow left-hander. The fact remained that Barrington did not play in anything like his true form and lost in straight games. Ken Hiscoe the second seed went down to the youthful Geoff Hunt, and in the final Hunt allowed Nancarrow but five points.

FIRST INTERNATIONAL CHAMPIONSHIPS
1967 in Australia

Team Event — played in Sydney

1. AUSTRALIA bt Great Britain 3-0, bt New Zealand 3-0, bt South Africa 3-0, bt India 3-0, bt Pakistan 3-0.
2. GREAT BRITAIN lost to New Zealand 1-2, bt South Africa 2-1, bt Pakistan 3-0, bt India 3-0.
3. NEW ZEALAND lost to South Africa 1-2, lost to Pakistan 1-2, bt India 2-1.
4. SOUTH AFRICA bt Pakistan 3-0, bt India 3-0.
5. PAKISTAN lost to India 1-2.
6. INDIA.

Individual Event — played in Melbourne

Third round: J. P. Barrington (GB) bt E. Hamilton (Australia) 9-0, 9-2, 9-2; D. Botha (SA) bt P. Dibley (NZ) 9-7, 5-9, 9-3, 4-9, 9-7; C. Nancarrow (Australia) bt C. Waugh (NZ) 9-7, 9-5, 9-7; R. Carter (Australia) bt R. Ratinac (Australia) 9-0, 10-8, 9-5; G. Hunt (Australia) bt T. Johnston (NZ) 9-0, 9-5, 9-1; M. W. Corby (GB) bt David Barrow (SA) 9-0, 9-1, 9-1; T. Burgess (Australia) bt T. Quick (Australia) 9-4, 9-7, 7-9, 9-7; K. Hiscoe (Australia) bt P. Stokes (GB) 9-1, 9-6, 10-8.

Quarter-finals: Barrington bt Botha 9-7, 10-9, 9-1; Nancarrow bt Carter 9-5, 7-9, 9-6, 3-9, 9-4; Hunt bt Corby 9-3, 9-3, 10-8; Hiscoe bt Burgess 9-5, 9-3, 9-3.

Semi-finals: Nancarrow bt Barrington 9-7, 9-6, 9-7; Hunt bt Hiscoe 9-3, 9-7, 0-9, 10-8.

Final: Hunt bt Nancarrow 9-3, 9-2, 9-0.

SECOND AND THIRD INTERNATIONAL CHAMPIONSHIPS

After the inaugural International Championships in Australia in 1967 it had been agreed that the next Championships should be held in Egypt in November 1968. With their wealth of professional talent, Egypt had obtained permission from the ISRF to add an Open Event but the troubled times in the Middle East caused the Egyptians to withdraw from being hosts. The 1967 General Meeting of the ISRF had laid down that the next Championships should be held, if not in Egypt, in either Pakistan or Great Britain, but after the withdrawal of Egypt, Pakistan stated that they were not ready. The Second Championships were accordingly held in England in February 1969, about a year and a half after the first Championships.

At this time, sponsorship of squash was in its infancy and the event was financed partly by a Government grant and partly by an appeal for contributions from firms connected with the game, and from individual members of the SRA. A raid was also made on the SRA International fund, financed mainly by contributions from the Dunlop Sports Company.

The Open Championship of the British Isles was held at the Abbeydale Sports Club, Sheffield, immediately before the commencement of the Team Event, and was used as a 'warming-up tournament' in order to enable the overseas teams to become acclimatised to the slow courts likely to be met during the winter in the Midlands.

The players in the Team Event were based on Birmingham with the headquarters at the Edgbaston-Priory Club. The matches were played on the courts of nine clubs. While some of these were in the suburbs of Birmingham matches were also arranged at centres, some as far as 50 miles away from Birmingham. It says much for the enthusiasm of players, officials, as well as of spectators, that the hazards of fog, snow and ice were all overcome successfully and all the matches took place on the stated dates, although not always on time. In particular the match at Nottingham, 50 miles from Birmingham, took place in a raging snow storm. Six teams took part — Australia, Great Britain, New Zealand, Pakistan, South Africa and the UAR. India were unable to get their Government's permission to compete.

The Team Event demonstrated once again the marked superiority of Australia over the rest of the world. Their team, again consisting of Hunt, Carter, Hiscoe and Nancarrow was undefeated, losing only three ties out of the 15 played. Great Britain represented by Jonah Barrington, Mike Corby, Don Innes and Paul Millman came second being beaten only by Australia, while the UAR failed to win a match. In view of later developments it is interesting to note that the South Africans competed in harmony with both Pakistan and the UAR and that the Socialist Government of the day had no objection to making a grant, knowing that a South African team would be competing. Britain lost 1-2 to Australia on the final night, their only win coming from Barrington who beat Geoff Hunt after two hours play by 9-7 in the fifth game, a result to be reversed only a few days later. Britain were perhaps fortunate to take second place as in the match against Pakistan, in the deciding tie, Barrington, playing Aftab Jawaid trailed 3-8 in the fifth game. In the second half of this last game Jawaid had two penalty points against him, the second being at match point.

There was universal approval of the holding of two major events — the British Open and the ISRF Team Event Championships in the provinces. Apart from the obvious point of showing the highest calibre of squash to a host of spectators who would never otherwise have had the opportunity of seeing it, the courts were cooler than in London and the squash was better, and therefore a better advertisement for the game than the hot house squash played in the courts of the Lansdowne and the RAC in London.

With the Team Event players only taking up 24 places there were 40 places in the draw open either to home players or overseas players who had not played in the Team Event. Whereas in 1967 in Australia Barrington and Hiscoe had been seeded to meet in the final, this time it was Barrington and Hunt. In the event Hunt won fairly conclusively after dropping the second game. The prizes were presented by HRH the Duke of Edinburgh who had honoured the SRA in a similar way in 1956 at the finals of the Open Championship.

SECOND CHAMPIONSHIPS
1969 in England

Results — Team Event

1. AUSTRALIA bt Great Britain 2-1, bt South Africa 2-1, bt Pakistan 2-1, bt Egypt 3-0, bt New Zealand 3-0.

2. GREAT BRITAIN bt South Africa 3-0, bt Pakistan 2-1, bt Egypt 2-1, bt New Zealand 2-1.

3. PAKISTAN bt South Africa 2-1, bt Egypt 3-0, bt New Zealand 2-1.

4. SOUTH AFRICA bt Egypt 2-1, bt New Zealand 2-1.

5. NEW ZEALAND bt Egypt 3-0.

6. EGYPT.

Individual Event — played at the Lansdowne Club, London

Third round: J. P. Barrington (GB) bt P. G. Kirton (GB) 9-1, 9-0, 9-3; T. Johnston (NZ) bt R. V. Lewis (Australia) 9-5, 9-2, 9-5; C. Nancarrow (Australia) bt G. Macdonald (SA) 9-7, 5-9, 5-9, 9-4, 9-4; R. Carter (Australia) bt J. Isaacs (NZ) 9-1, 9-2, 9-0; M. W. Corby (GB) bt P. G. Richards (GB) 9-5, 9-5, 9-6; K. Hiscoe (Australia) bt D. Burmeister (NZ) 9-3, 9-1, 9-4; A. A. Jawaid (Pakistan) bt D. Broom (SA) 7-9, 9-3, 9-0, 4-9, 9-6; G. Hunt (Australia) bt M. Saleem (Pakistan) 9-2, 9-2, 9-3.

Quarter-finals: Barrington bt Johnston 9-7, 9-1, 9-2; Nancarrow bt Carter 10-8, 9-7, 9-7; Hiscoe bt Corby 9-7, 9-5, 9-6; Hunt bt Jawaid 9-5, 9-2, 9-2.

Semi-finals: Barrington bt Nancarrow 9-0, 9-2, 10-8; Hunt bt Hiscoe 9-6, 9-5, 2-9, 9-7.

Final: Hunt bt Barrington 9-7, 2-9, 9-4, 9-0.

THIRD CHAMPIONSHIPS
1971 in New Zealand

It had been decided at the 1969 meeting of the ISRF that the next Championships should be played in New Zealand and there were no untoward events to alter this decision. Once again the two events were held in different parts of the country, but both were played in the North Island. The Team Event matches were played at Palmerston North, Henderson and Remuera with the Individual Event played at Hamilton. Seven teams took part including India and Canada, who had not competed in 1969 but excluding South Africa whose entry had been objected to by India. This was the first time a Transatlantic team had taken part. Unfortunately but predictably their enthusiasm was not matched by their performance. Australia continued to dominate the Team Event winning all their matches while Great Britain came second after a triple tie with Pakistan and Egypt; but Great Britain won more ties than the other two.

The final tally was:

	Matches Won	Ties Won	Points
1. AUSTRALIA	6	17	6
2. GREAT BRITAIN	4	13	4
3. PAKISTAN	4	12	4
4. EGYPT	4	11	4
5. NEW ZEALAND	2	6	2
6. INDIA	1	3	1
7. CANADA	0	1	0

The Individual Event was played at Hamilton which boasted a fine new court with a viewing capacity of 250. With Barrington now a professional, Australia dominated this event more than ever, three of the top four seeds being Australian. These four duly reached the semi-finals which resulted in an all-Australian final between Hunt and Nancarrow. This was a replay of the 1967 final, but where on that occasion Nancarrow won only seven points, this time he did better and unexpectedly won the third game after Hunt had led 8-1.

At the meeting of the ISRF held during the Championships in New Zealand a decision on the venue of the next Championships was not reached.

Individual Event

Third round: G. Hunt (Australia) bt P. Handa (India) 9-5, 9-5, 9-1; A. Jawaid (Pakistan) bt W. Reedman (Australia) 9-3, 9-3, 9-0; K. Hiscoe (Australia) bt G. Allam (Egypt) 9-4, 9-1, 9-2; J. Easter (GB) bt A. Kaoud (Egypt) 9-3, 9-2, 9-3; R. Lewis (Australia) bt M. Saleem (Pakistan) 5-9, 9-0, 9-4, 9-7; M. Asran (Egypt) bt M. Helal (Egypt) 9-0, 9-4, 9-2; P. Ayton (GB) bt A. Ispahani (India) 9-6, 9-1, 9-4; C. Nancarrow (Australia) bt M. Corby (GB) 9-6, 9-3, 9-5.

Quarter-finals: Hunt bt Jawaid 5-9, 9-6, 9-6, 9-7; Hiscoe bt Easter 9-4, 9-7, 9-5; Asran bt Lewis 9-3, 9-7, 9-7; Nancarrow bt Ayton 2-9, 10-9, 9-2, 9-7.

Semi-finals: Hunt bt Hiscoe 9-1, 9-3, 3-9, 9-1; Nancarrow bt Asran 9-5, 6-9, 9-7, 9-5.

Final: Hunt bt Nancarrow 9-6, 9-7, 8-10, 9-5.

Play-off for third place: Hiscoe bt Asran 9-5, 9-3, 9-2.

Plate final: Mohibullah (Pakistan) bt C. Waugh (NZ) 9-5, 10-8, 9-0.

FOURTH CHAMPIONSHIPS
1973 in South Africa

The venue of future championships was a regular and disputatious item on the agenda of every meeting of the ISRF. At the meeting held in New Zealand in 1971, Pakistan wished it to be confirmed that the next Championships should be played in their country, but added, ominously, that the Pakistan Government would not consent to all members of the Federation being invited. Several other countries appeared willing to host this Championship and the South African delegate stated that his Government had categorically informed him that all Members of the Federation would be allowed to enter South Africa and play in the Championships if held there. Several delegates referred to communication difficulties with the national federation of Pakistan. The final resolution carried declared that the next Championships should go to Pakistan provided that an assurance had been received by a due date that every Member could be invited to compete. It was also decided that in the event of this assurance not having been received, the Championships should go to South Africa providing that the country had signified its willingness to invite every Member of the Federation. This gave Pakistan six months to get its Government to effect a major change of policy in order that South Africa could be invited. It was realised by all that this was extremely unlikely and in the event, the required assurance having been received from South Africa, and in the absence of a similar assurance from Pakistan, by early March 1972, South Africa was given the go ahead to organise the Championships in August 1973. This did not give the SRA of South Africa very long to organise the Championships but they made a splendid job of it and the team event was commenced in

Johannesburg on August 15, 1973. The Individual Championships were played near Durban at Cabana Beach and the Durban Country Club from August 30 to September 8. In spite of the South African invitation to the coloured members of the Federation there were no competitors from Egypt, Pakistan, India and surprisingly at the last minute, Canada. The gap created by the late withdrawal of Canada was plugged by a scratch side, called the International side, and composed of overseas players who were either omitted from their country's teams or whose countries had not sent a team (Holland), and in both cases had entered for the Individual event. The countries competing in the Team Event were: Australia, Great Britain, South Africa, New Zealand and the USA, and this was the order in which they were placed at the conclusion of the event. Australia retained the Team Trophy which they had held since the event was first played in 1967, but by the closest of margins. Great Britain was second but had Stuart Courtney, their second string won one of the two match points he held over the Australian, Mike Donnelly, Great Britain would have won the match and the Championship.

Team Event
The results of the Team Event, the matches of which were played in and around Johannesburg were:
1. AUSTRALIA bt Great Britain 2-1, bt South Africa 2-1, bt New Zealand 3-0, bt USA 3-0.
2. GREAT BRITAIN bt South Africa 2-1, bt New Zealand 3-0, bt USA 3-0.
3. SOUTH AFRICA bt New Zealand 3-0, bt USA 3-0.
4. NEW ZEALAND bt USA 3-0.
5. USA.
The Individual event consisted of 20 players who had competed in the Team Event, the remaining 44 being either home players or overseas players eligible to complete. The absence of Hunt and Hiscoe who had turned professional since the last Championships did not seem to have diminished the Australian domination of this event, three of the semi-finalists being Australian. The hero of the event was undoubtedly Britain's Brian Patterson who, unseeded, reached the final by beating the second seed, Doug Wright, but he was no match in the final for Australia's Cam Nancarrow who, as had become the custom, turned professional immediately after winning.
The final rounds were played at Cabana Beach which at that time boasted the only glass back walls in Africa.

Individual Event
Third round: C. Nancarrow (Australia) bt S. Courtney (GB) 9-7, 10-8, 9-3; W. Reedman (Australia) bt S. Sherren (SA) 9-5, 9-6, 9-2; P. Ayton (GB) bt K. Coppin (SA) 9-3, 7-9, 10-8, 9-6; M. Donnelly (Australia) bt D. Botha (SA) 9-4, 9-6, 10-8; B. Patterson (GB) bt R.

Watson (SA) 6-9, 9-6, 9-7, 9-6; J. Easter (GB) bt D. Barrow (SA) 10-8, 5-9, 2-9, 9-5, 9-5; L. Robberds (Australia) bt D. Quail (SA) 9-0, 9-6, 9-2; D. Wright (Australia) bt M. Watson (SA) 9-6, 9-4, 9-4.

Quarter-finals: Nancarrow bt Reedman 5-9, 9-3, 9-5, 10-8; Donnelly bt Ayton 3-9, 10-8, 9-2, 10-8; Patterson bt Easter 9-4, 10-8, 9-1; Wright bt Robberds 9-4, 9-10, 9-4, 9-5.

Semi-finals: Nancarrow bt Donnelly 10-9, 9-3, 7-9, 9-6; Patterson bt Wright 5-9, 9-5, 9-7, 10-8.

Final: Nancarrow bt Patterson 9-2, 9-5, 9-1.

Play-off for third place: Wright bt Donnelly 5-9, 4-9, 9-5, 9-2, 9-3.

FIFTH CHAMPIONSHIPS
1976 in England

The choice of venue for the fifth International Championships was the subject of endless debate at the General Meetings of 1973 and 1975. At the 1971 General Meeting it had been agreed that the 1975 Championships should go to Canada. When the matter came up for discussion at the 1973 meeting South Africa's representative stated that if invited by the Canadians to compete, his country would certainly accept, but it was also clear that South African participation would result in the withdrawal of the coloured countries. The Canadian delegate offered that his country would step down in favour of Egypt or India or Pakistan provided that the following Championship should go to Canada. It was finally decided that the Championships should be offered firstly to Egypt, secondly to Pakistan and thirdly to Canada in the spring of 1976.

In the event, both Egypt and Pakistan intimated their inability to host the Championships and Canada decided that she would not be able to have the Championships in 1976 immediately before the Olympic Games due to be played in that country in July 1976. Other countries were approached but the only offer came from Great Britain. It was therefore decided at the 1975 General Meeting that the Championships should be held in England in May 1976.

Although given less than a year to organise the Championships the SRA managed this, although with a minimum of sponsorship. As in 1969 when the Championships were last played in England the Team Event was played in the Midlands with the teams based on Birmingham, followed by the Individual Event at Wembley. There was a good deal of political infighting before South Africa was persuaded to withdraw from the Team Event. Had they not done so, Egypt, India, Pakistan, Kuwait and Nigeria would have been forced to withdraw by their respective Governments and, worse, the British Government made it clear that they would not contribute any grant, without which it would not have been possible to organise the Championships. It was decided however that South Africans could compete as individuals at Wembley.

There was a record entry of 11 teams making it necessary, for the first time, to divide the teams into two pools. There was a sensational start when on the first day the Nigerian team was ordered to withdraw by the office of the Nigerian High Commissioner in London under the mistaken impression that a South African team was competing. Fortunately Nigeria was in the pool containing six teams so that by their withdrawal each pool consisted of an even number of teams.

The two leading teams in Pool A (Australia and Egypt) and in Pool B (Great Britain and Pakistan) played a round robin to decide the Team Championship, from which for the first time Great Britain emerged as winners. The remaining countries in both pools also played a round robin as a result of which the order of merit came out as follows:

1. Great Britain
2. Pakistan
3. Australia
4. Egypt
5. New Zealand
6. Sweden
7. India
8. Canada
9. USA
10. Kuwait

The Individual Event for which 73 players were accepted by the SRA (nine more than provided for in the Rules governing Amateur International Championships) was again won by an Australian, Kevin Shawcross who, in the final, beat third seeded David Scott from South Africa. Six of the Afro-Asian countries players withdrew when they came up against South African players, acting on the instructions of their Governments. Scott made a fine effort in the final in taking Shawcross to five games, incidentally providing the first final of this event to go the full distance. As had become customary the winner announced immediately after the final that he was turning professional. Both the Plate and the Classic Plate were won by South Africans against Swedes, providing yet another example of the rapid increase in the standard of Sweden's top players.

Individual Event

Third round: K. Shawcross (Australia) bt J. C. A. Leslie (GB) 9-4, 9-4, 9-3; N. Barbour (NZ) bt M. W. Corby (GB) 9-5, 9-4, 8-1, retired; B. Brownlee (NZ) bt S. H. Courtney (GB) 8-10, 9-3, 9-6, 9-0; M. Donnelly (Australia) bt G. Stanier (SA) 3-9, 9-2, 9-3, 9-4; L. Keppell (Australia) bt L. Kvant (Sweden) 9-2, 9-7, 9-2; D. Scott (SA) w/o Maqsood Ahmed; I. Holding (SA) bt H. Brown (NZ) 9-7, 5-9, 9-7, 9-4; P. N. Ayton (GB) bt A. Colborn (SA) 2-9, 9-3, 1-9, 9-1, 9-4.

Quarter-finals: Shawcross bt Barbour 9-5, 9-1, 9-4; Donnelly bt Brownlee 5-9, 9-7, 9-0, 9-0; Scott bt Keppell 9-7, 9-4, 9-4; Holding bt

167

Ayton 9-1, 9-3, 5-9, 9-6.

Semi-finals: Shawcross bt Donnelly 9-3, 9-4, 9-2; Scott bt Holding 2-9, 9-3, 9-10, 9-6, 9-2.

Final: Shawcross bt Scott 9-1, 0-9, 9-6, 6-9, 9-2.

Classic Plate final: R. Colburn (SA) bt L. Kvant (Sweden) 9-6, 8-10, 9-6, 6-9, 9-3.

Plate final: R. O'Connor (SA) bt T. Tovar (Sweden) 9-0, 10-8, 9-4.

SIXTH CHAMPIONSHIPS
1977 in Canada

These were held in Canada in September 1977 and once again were saved by the undertaking of South Africa not to compete. Only eight nations competed — four fewer than in 1976, which made it unnecessary to divide the teams into two pools. The matches of the Team Event were played at clubs in and around Ottawa while the Individual Event was played at the Bridlewood Squash Club at Toronto. For the first time an International Veterans Championship was included and which attracted an entry of 18 players. It had originally been decided that there should also be a doubles championship which was to have been played in New York but the USSRA finally withdrew their offer to host this event because they had not been informed sufficiently early that South Africa was not to be represented. Had South Africans been competing, other African and Asian teams would have withdrawn. The sponsors of this event had set a deadline which was reached before the ISRF informed the USSRA that South Africa would not be competing.

The Team Event provided the closest finish in the history of the Championships with Pakistan, New Zealand and Egypt all ending up with six wins but the complicated scoring system finally provided that Pakistan were declared the winners with New Zealand second and Egypt third. The holders, Great Britain could manage no better than fourth place.

In the Individual Event, Pakistan players dominated the play and Bruce Brownlee the New Zealander who having won the British Amateur Championship the preceding January, was made top seed, but was beaten by the eighth seeded M. Saleem, a Pakistani. The final was between two brothers, Saleem and Maqsood, with the latter several years the younger, winning easily. The Classic Plate was an all New Zealand affair, their players filling three of the semi-final places and providing both finalists. The Veterans Championship was won by Harry O'Connor, a white player from Zambia.

The final order of placings in the Team Event was:

1. Pakistan
2. New Zealand

3. Egypt
4. Great Britain
5. Australia
6. Sweden
7. Canada
8. USA

Individual Event

Third round: B. Brownlee (NZ) bt M. Desaulniers (Canada) 9-0, 2-9, 10-8, 10-8; M. Saleem (Pakistan) bt A. Soliman (Egypt) 8-9, 9-7, 9-3, 9-3; G. Awad (Egypt) bt F. Donnelly (Australia) 9-6, 9-1, 9-3; Atlas Khan (Pakistan) bt M. Lilley (NZ) 9-6, 4-9, 7-9, 9-5, 9-0; L. Kvant (Sweden) bt I. Robinson (GB) 9-1, 9-1, 4-9, 9-7; Maqsood Ahmed (Pakistan) bt M. Awad (Egypt) 9-5, 9-4, 9-1; D. Williams (Australia) bt H. Broun (NZ) 7-9, 9-3, 1-9, 9-3, 9-6; J. C. Leslie (GB) bt Daulas Khan (Pakistan) 9-4, 10-8, 9-6.

Fouth round: Saleem bt Brownlee 10-8, 4-9, 9-5, 3-9, 9-1; G. Awad bt Atlas Khan 9-6, 9-0, 9-5; Maqsood bt Kvant 9-0, 9-1, 9-4; Leslie bt Williams 9-2, 6-9, 9-1, 9-0.

Semi-finals: Saleem bt G. Awad 9-7, 9-4, 2-9, 9-7; Maqsood bt Leslie 6-9, 9-2, 2-9, 9-5, 9-3.

Final: Maqsood bt Saleem 9-3, 9-7, 9-4.

Classic Plate final: M. Lilley (NZ) bt H. Broun (NZ) 9-6, 6-9, 9-1, 7-9, 9-6.

Veterans Championship final: H. O'Connor (Zambia) bt D. Green (NZ) 9-7, 9-7, 9-1.

CHAPTER XII

AMATEUR STATUS

*T*HE QUESTION of amateur status had bedevilled squash only in the last few years. Since the quite early days of the game there have been professionals, generally attached to schools (where they were primarily rackets professionals) or, at clubs, quite frequently lawn tennis clubs where they were engaged as lawn tennis professionals. In England, squash professionals, as such, first made their appearance in the London West End clubs. Most of them had started their professional careers as ball boys at Queens or Princes Clubs. They were keen and dedicated, preferring the life of a sports professional which brought little in the form of pecuniary reward. Unlike their fellow pros, at lawn tennis, they did not enjoy the benefits of working mainly in the open air.

When the game began to expand seriously in the fifties and sixties the demand for professionals far outstripped the supply in England. Suddenly there appeared the Pakistanis and the Egyptians. Many came to England as amateur players subsidised by their national associations or by clubs. Others, having been professionals in their own country, were attracted by the increasing payments being made to pros, and by the high standard of living in England compared with their own countries. Finally came sponsorship in various forms which resulted in a large increase in the prize money for professional events, and which was the direct cause of a number of the best amateur players in the world turning professional.

The Squash Rackets Association for many years did not think it necessary to include in the Constitution of the Association any reference to a definition of amateur status. But the dissolution of the Squash Rackets Professionals Association in 1938 and the transfer of its members to the Squash Rackets Association altered the situation and in 1939 "Definition of amateur status" was added to the Rules of the SRA. Curiously the rule did not define who was an amateur but who was a professional. The latter was one who had received money for playing or teaching squash rackets. Immediately after the war an addition to the rule laid down how and in what circumstances a professional could regain his amateur status. This rule worked well for a number of years but in 1964 the growing shortage of professionals and the increasing demand for instructors led the SRA to set up a sub committee to study the question of coaching. The outcome was the establishment of courses and examinations for amateur coaches. The first, held in September 1964 at the Crystal Palace was a much greater success than the organisers had anticipated and the list of those attending the course had to be closed at 50. Of these, 21 passed the subsequent examinations and became the first Approved Amateur Coaches. It was thought that provision should be made, as an encouragement, for these coaches to be entitled to receive under carefully regulated conditions, some remuneration without forfeiting their amateur status. This was incorporated in a new draft of Rule 5 which under the same heading laid down what constituted an amateur. The new rule was bitterly criticised by the SRA of Australia who insisted that such pseudo amateurs should not be permitted to play in the Amateur Championship or in the Amateur Veterans Championship if they had received payment for coaching. At that time the SRAA was affiliated to the SRA and the latter rather grudgingly gave in.

There was never any intention by the SRA of permitting any clash between professional and amateur coaches. Any approved amateur coach who wanted to receive payment had to obtain prior approval from the SRA who before granting it required full details and only gave their permission if they were convinced that no professional coaching was obtainable.

It is apposite at this stage to examine the question of what professional coaching was available in England at the time. In 1964 there were only 58 professional members of the SRA practising as such in England. Of these 27 were attached to clubs and were not usually permitted by their employers to coach other than club members. A further seven were attached to schools and probably augmented their salaries with coaching done in the vacations. Of the remaining 24 which were classed as "unattached" only five were full time squash pros, the remainder being lawn tennis professionals who were happy to earn extra cash by teaching squash as well. The original definition of amateur status specifically laid down that a player who had forfeited his amateur status at any other racket game could not compete as an amateur at squash.

The Professionals Committee of the SRA laid down standards for their members who on election were expected to pass an examination on their ability to play, to coach and to mark. But this was not in the early days obligatory and many coaches at lawn tennis who wanted to advertise themselves as registered squash rackets coaches merely had to pay the small annual subscription. This state of affairs was obviously unsatisfactory and the Professionals Committee in 1963 decided to create three categories of professional membership. On election a professional became a Provisional Member. He was expected to take the examination for Full Membership within a year. Should he fail his examination or without due cause fail to take the examination he became an Associate Member. This last category, the lowest form, was of considerable use to the Pakistanis whose command of English was often not sufficient to enable them to pass such an exam. But most of those who had been professional members before were automatically granted Full Membership although many of them would not have passed the exam if they had been required to do so.

It is obvious from the figures quoted above that the number of professional coaches was entirely inadequate for the work of teaching the rapidly expanding game. A further cause for concern was the small number of professional recruits, and particularly young men. Most of the Full Members in 1964 had been professionals before the war. There has in the past 10 years been some improvement in this respect. Of the 58 professional members practising in England in 1964, seven were Pakistanis.

In 1973 the position had improved and the total number of Professional members practising in this country had risen to 90 — an increase of 55%. By 1978 membership had risen to 147 (including 16 women) of which number 21 (mostly Pakistanis, had been imported from overseas. The majority of the members were practising in England, but 12 had obtained employment outside this country. But even this percentage is probably no greater than the percentage increase in the numbers playing the game. All of which is surely a vindication of the SRA policy of introducing approved amateur coaches.

The original figure of 21 Approved Amateur Coaches in 1964 had risen by 1976 to 206. This figure does not include 48 who have passed the exam but live outside England. Not all of the Approved Amateur Coaches have accepted fees for coaching. A large number are schoolmasters who wanted to improve their coaching methods. A lower standard of coaching was required for a further class of Elementary Coaches, nearly 500 of which had been awarded their SRA certificate by 1976.

There is no doubt that in the last few years there has grown into the game — and not only in England — a certain amount of 'shamateurism' which all but destroyed lawn tennis. The proliferation of tournaments plus sponsorship has been mainly responsible. The SRA laid down — though it does not appear in the Rules of the SRA — that no amateur should be rewarded with a prize or voucher worth more than £50. This figure has since been raised to £100. One overseas player, having been presented with a voucher for this amount, promptly walked over to the bar and cashed it! Sponsors naturally want to attract the best players to their tournaments and to do this proudly announce ever increasing sums as prize money. This is fair enough where open tournaments are concerned but can they be blamed if, being limited to a £50 prize voucher, they find some other means of adding to the attraction of their tournaments? The SRA was well aware of the hypocracy of the situation and at two successive meetings of the ISRF put forward resolutions to abolish amateur status. This would have been a realistic way out of the difficulty but the proposal was strongly opposed on each occasion by Australia. This was perhaps not surprising for Australia's amateur status rule is longer and more restrictive than that of any other country. When Geoff Hunt came as an amateur in the early seventies to play a series of matches against Jonah Barrington, already a professional, his daily expenses were paid to the SRA by the sponsoring company and then had to be handed personally to Geoff by an official at Australia House. As for the air fare and expenses of Geoff's wife, ineligible under the Australian amateur rule — well perhaps we should draw a veil! Another aspect of the Australian amateur rule limits an amateur to the number of consecutive weeks overseas he can play. An Australian amateur also has to obtain the permission of his national or State association to play in amateur tournaments outside Australia. It was the refusal of the SRA of Australia to allow Billie Reedman to play in the International Amateur Championships in South Africa (he was not selected as a member of the Australian official team) which decided Reedman to turn pro.

The ISRF has always been under pressure to lay down an amateur status rule which would be binding on every member. A sensible rule was adopted to cover the Amateur International Championships which ran as follows:

"An amateur squash rackets player is a person who plays or teaches the game solely for pleasure, recreation or honour without seeking or obtaining from it financial gain, directly or indirectly either for himself or another".

This is, in fact, the first sentence of the Australian Rule. It was what came after this simple definition which convinced the 1971 General Meeting of the ISRF that agreement and enforcement of a rule would not be possible worldwide. And so this simple definition of amateur status was inserted in the Championship Rules only.

National prestige in sport is looked upon as important by many governments. How far some governments will go in their efforts to achieve this is the crux of the matter. In squash, the chief amateur players in Pakistan spend their whole time living at 'squash camps' where they do nothing but play squash. Presumably they receive free board and lodging. They are on the payroll of PIA. There are many who feel that the amateur status of these players should be at risk.

The United States SRA under its Rules of Eligibility starts off with the same definition as that adopted by the ISRF for their International Championship Rules and then, rather like the Australians, enlarges on this with what are called 'Specific Rules'.

One of the main difficulties in the past has been the attitude of national squash associations towards those who are acknowledged professionals at other sports. The original definition adopted by the SRA specifically prohibited professionals at other racket games from competing as amateurs at squash — "No one who has forfeited his amateur status at any other racket game shall be eligible to play squash rackets as an amateur". There can be no doubt that the SRA had in mind rackets professionals. In the early days the teaching of rackets and squash was frequently done by the same professional and it appeared unfair that a rackets professional should be able to compete against amateurs at squash. But "any other racket game" must have included lawn tennis. Why should a lawn tennis professional be unable to play in amateur squash competitions, when such a ban did not exist on professional footballers? When the new amateur rule was adopted in 1966 this anomaly was dropped. In the US Rules of Eligibility it is specifically laid down that ineligibility at any other sport is not of itself a ban to playing squash as an amateur.

Another important aspect of this question is the attitude of other countries when a national association declares one of its players to be suspended as an amateur. When in 1970 the Australian Association suspended Rainer Ratinac because of his association with a touring 'circus' which included professionals, the SRA accepted the situation and Ratinac did not play in that season's Amateur Championship in England. But then came the Muneer case when the Pakistan SRF in November 1971 wrote to the SRA stating that they had suspended S. Muneer and asking that he should be barred from taking part in amateur tournaments. The SRA replied by enquiring what Muneer had done to merit suspension, but this information was not forthcoming. The SRA accordingly refused the Pakistan request and Muneer continued to compete in our tournaments. His suspension which had political undertones was subsequently lifted by the Pakistan SRA.

Although the ISRF were not directly involved in this dispute the wider issues involved prompted that body to question their members on what if anything should be done. Few took the opportunity of stating their view.

Every meeting of the ISRF debated the question of amateur status in some form or another.

At the 1977 ISRF General Meeting it was the Swedes who tabled a resolution proposing that the game should go 'open' "within a few years" and for the first time the Federation took a positive step in that direction by agreeing to Sweden forming a committee with the task of "reviewing the current amateur rule and the *possible transition to open squash*" (my italics). It was rightly felt that it would be quicker if all the members of the committee came from the same country but that the views of all members of the ISRF should be sought. The meeting hoped that the Swedes would be ready to complete their report by the end of June 1978 but this did not prove possible but Great Britain has now put forward a motion to be debated at the October 1979 meeting of the ISRF that the game should go 'open' in 1981, but it remains to be seen whether this will command sufficient support to get passed.

At the same 1977 ISRF meeting Great Britain and Finland put forward yet another definition of amateur status, which was carried but not by a sufficient majority to enable it to become operative. However, a few months later an amended version of the same rule was submitted to a postal vote of members of the ISRF and this time obtained the necessary majority. Unfortunately it merely defined an amateur player, omitted all mention of sections of the existing rule governing allowances for board and accommodation, approved amateur coaches, forfeiture of amateur status etc. So utter confusion reigned but with the Swedish report expected to favour the abolition of amateur status, no action was taken to straighten matters out.

The Womens SRA, bolder than their male counterpart and tired of the endless delays which have bedevilled decisions on the subject by the ISRF decided, boldly, in the autumn of 1978 to abolish all distinctions between amateur and professionals under their jurisdiction.

When the Swedish SRA's report was eventually received early in 1979 it was found to contain recommendations that the game and its development should be controlled and administered by the ISRF and the regional Squash Rackets Federations in co-operation with organisations such as the International Squash Players Association (the professional players), the Womens Squash Players Association and other organisations and that these should include womens squash, and that all categories of players should be controlled and administered by the ISRF and its sattelite bodies. Also that players who wanted to, should be able to earn money from their squash, but should be able to do so within the activities of the ISRF.

It is obvious that the proposals will be the subject of much debate by members of the ISRF, and resolutions embodying these recommendations are due to be debated at the 1979 meeting of the ISRF.

CHAPTER XIII

SQUASH LITERATURE

*I*N COMMON with the haphazard beginnings of the game, it was a long time before any books were written about squash. The oldest book on record is a slim volume of 116 pages in the All England Series published in 1901 by E. H. Miles. The same author in the following year wrote a more ambitious volume on racquets, tennis and squash. Seven years later the first book appeared in the United States — "Court Tennis, with Notes on Racquets and Squash Racquets". Squash was included in a few books in England mainly concerned with other sports prior to 1914 and the outbreak of war effectively stopped further books on the game. Charles Arnold, one of the 'Three Musketeers' of professional squash (the others were Read and Johnson) who as professional at the Bath Club taught the Prince of Wales and other members of the Royal Family in the twenties and thirties, was a natural to burst into print and his "The Game of Squash Racquets" was published in 1926 and was a modest volume of 64 pages. Note the spelling 'racquets' and compare with another book published in the same year: "The Field Handbook of Squash Rackets" by E. B. Noel, father of Susan who later became one of the most famous of women players. Arnold's book was the last to be published in this country with the old spelling of the game. Only in America is the spelling with 'QU' continued to the present day, and the reluctance of Americans to adopt the spelling used by the rest of the world is alleged to be the unsavoury definition of 'racket' common in America. The second of the 'Three Musketeers', Charles Read, wrote the first full length instructional book on the game (153 pages) in 1929.

The first amateur in England to break into print was Amr Bey who wrote in 1934 with the authority of being both Open and Amateur Champion, and the increasing popularity of the game in the second half of the thirties led to a rash of books on the game, mostly small, but mention should be made of Susan Noel's book of 110 pages in 1937 which was aimed principally at women players.

Volume 16 of the Lonsdale Library published in 1933 and edited by the late Lord Aberdare dealt in detail with Rackets, Squash Rackets, Tennis, Fives and Badminton, and in addition to valuable instructional chapters contained a fascinating history of ball games, including an authoritative description of the beginnings of squash.

After the 1939-45 War a number of publishing houses producing sports series added squash, with leading amateurs as well as professionals engaged to write the books. When the leading newspapers started to employ squash correspondents, Rex Bellamy of "The Times" emerged as the most gifted writer on the game. Squash professionals cannot normally be expected to be gifted writers and so a combination of Rex Bellamy and Leslie Hamer, one of the best professionals in the game, produced in 1968 a readable and instructive little volume in the Teach Yourself series published by the English Universities Press.

The most prolific writer on the game is R. B. Hawkey whose many volumes for various series of sports books for more than one publisher have shown originality and have avoided repetition. Mr Hawkey's qualifications for writing on squash are considerable for apart from being an ex-international player, he has combined the experience gained from his profession of a schoolmaster with that of Director of Coaching for the SRA.

To have the greatest names in sport writing books for them is the dream of every publisher, but proficiency in sport is not always allied to proficiency with the pen and ghost writers frequently are employed to bridge the gap. Hashim Khan, perhaps the greatest name in the history of squash, and resident for many years in the USA, has written with the aid of Richard Randall the most entertaining book on squash which is set down in the actual words of Hashim, in that unique type of half-English, which has come to be known as Hashimese.

Jonah Barrington the most celebrated of all British players started his literary career with a book which owed as much to his literary agent as to Jonah, but subsequently showed that he could write as well as play squash — Jonah is also an excellent speaker and like many Irishmen, never at a loss for words. Geoff Hunt is another great player who can write well but the Egyptian Dardir needed the literary help of Garth Gilmour to produce one of the best instructional books on the game. Dardir has recently written a second book, edited by New Zealander Brian Humberstone.

Annuals started making their appearance in the thirties and the first of these was the Squash Rackets Association Handbook first published in 1929/30, a slim volume in those days, while in 1936 a much larger work "The Squash Rackets Annual" edited by Hubert Winterbotham made its debut. The latter did not survive the War but the SRA Handbook has been published annually since 1947/8 when it contained 67 pages. The 1977/8 edition contained 519 pages. The latest body to produce an annual is the International Squash Rackets Federation which produced its first Handbook in 1975/6.

Before the War "Squash Rackets and Fives" was published monthly but this folded up in 1939 and its was not until 1948 that squash was added to the already established "British Lawn Tennis" and was quickly adopted as the official journal of the SRA. In 1972 this magazine decided to discontinue squash.

In 1969, however, a new entirely squash magazine was published *"Squash Rackets News"* which in November 1970 became the official journal of the SRA. This was taken over a year later by ACM WEBB (Publishers) Co Ltd who re-launched "Squash Rackets News" in an entirely new format as a monthly colour magazine called *"The Squash Player International"*, which is still published monthly as the official journal of the SRA and which has proved to be the most consistent and most successful of all squash periodicals published in the post-War years.

Overseas the USSRA and the Metropolitan SRA of New York have published annuals for many years. "Racquets — Canada", a monthly devotes a certain amount of space to squash. "Tennis SA and Squash" caters for the game in South Africa and Sweden has its own squash magazine — "Squash Nytto". Australia also has a monthly magazine.

INDEX

180

181